Praise for *Rip-Off*

"Crime can be fun, especially for those writing about it. Maybe the best thing about *Rip-Off* is the playfulness Faron brings to explaining the shadowy world of bunco artists. Sprinkled with real-life cases and leavened with wry humor, Faron's book shows the often inventive, always bold swindles grifters use to turn otherwise frugal, careful people into saps."   —Dan Reed, *San Jose Mercury News*

"Fay has the ability to describe every conceivable scam in simple, understandable terms, enabling the reader to view the world of deception in a clearer fashion. Fay's experience as an investigator and writer provide her with the ability to offer special insight into this world."
                    —Richard W. Smith, 25-year veteran of the FBI
                            and president of Cannon Street, Inc.,
                                    a private investigative firm

"Everything you need to know about the people you don't want to know. Not only is this a great A to Z 'Howdunit' for writers, it's also a must-buy manual for those whose job it is to go after the bad guys."
                    —Laurel Pallock, consumer protection investigator
                    and host of Bay TV's daily show, "All Consuming"

Praise for *Howdunit* Series
from Writer's Digest Books

"Essential buys for the serious author . . . will cut research time in half."   —*Mystery Scene Magazine*

"Read the entire volume of *Howdunit* books, and embarking on a life of crime seems a definite possibility."
                                    —*The Washington Post*

THE HOWDUNIT SERIES

RIP-OFF

a writer's guide to crimes of deception

Fay Faron

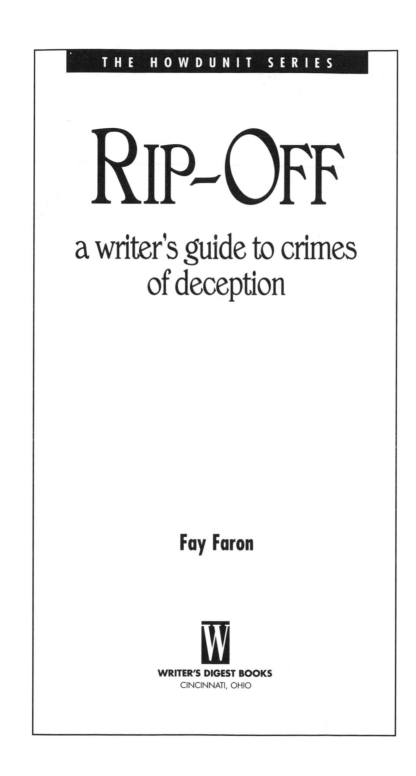

WRITER'S DIGEST BOOKS
CINCINNATI, OHIO

Dedication

To Jerry Faron, whose motto is,

"I give everybody a chance for ten years.
After that I write them off."

Rip-Off. Copyright © 1998 by Fay Faron. Manufactured in the United States of America. All rights reserved. No part of this book may be reproduced in any form or by any electronic or mechanical means including information storage and retrieval systems without permission in writing from the publisher, except by a reviewer, who may quote brief passages in a review. Published by Writer's Digest Books, an imprint of F&W Publications, Inc., 1507 Dana Ave., Cincinnati, Ohio 45207. (800) 289-0963. First edition.

Other fine Writer's Digest Books are available from your local bookstore or direct from the publisher.

02   01   00   99   98   5   4   3   2   1

Library of Congress Cataloging-in-Publication Data

Faron, Fay.
    Rip-off / by Fay Faron.—1st. ed.
        p.   cm.
    Includes bibliographical references and index.
    ISBN 0-89879-827-2 (pbk.:alk. paper)
    1. Fraud investigation—United States. 2. Swindlers and swindling—United States. 3. Deception—United States. I. Title. II. Title: Writers guide to crimes of deception.
    HV8079.F7F37   1998
    363.25'963—dc21   98-26096
                                                                              CIP

Content edited by Jack Heffron and John Kachuba
Production edited by Amanda Magoto
Cover illustration by Chris Spollen

About the Author

Through her extensive work as a detective, author, columnist and crusader, Fay Faron has firmly established herself as an investigative authority, specializing in missing persons cases and confidence schemes.

Most recently, Faron received national recognition for cracking San Francisco's notorious "Foxglove" case, which she brought to the attention of police. The alleged murder-for-profit scheme involved six elderly victims who were fleeced of their cash and subsequently poisoned. For her participation in this case, Faron was nominated for an Edgar Award by The Foundation for the Improvement of Justice. Her role in the case has also been featured in *Vanity Fair* and the book, *Hastened to the Grave*.

Among her other accomplishments, Faron's previous *Howdunit* book, *Missing Persons* was also nominated for an Edgar Award, and her long-runnning syndicated column "Ask Rat Dog" currently appears in more than forty newspapers, including *The Chicago Sun Times* and *The Dallas Morning News*.

As an expert in the field, Faron has appeared on *The Oprah Winfrey Show*, *Good Morning America* and *Larry King Live*, and she has also been featured in *Newsweek*, *USA Today*, *Money* and *Entrepreneur*, among several other publications.

Currently, Faron continues to work as a PI for her own Rat Dog Dick Detective Agency in San Francisco, where she is writing her first mystery novel, *Lily Kills Her Client*.

Acknowledgments

Thanks to Kate Cleary, executive director of the California Adoption Alliance; Joseph P. Davidson, Special Agent with the FBI's Organized Crime Division; Ann Flaherty, chief investigator of the Rat Dog Dick Detective Agency; Jon Grow, National Association of Bunco Investigators; Ed Hooks, actor/teacher/author and columnist of *Callboard* magazine's "Inside the Industry" column; Detective Sergeant Roy House (retired) of the Houston PD's Swindle Detail; J.J. Jacobson, investigator with the California Department of Insurance, Fraud Division; Leslie Kim, publisher of the *John Cooke Insurance Fraud Report*; Detective Joe Livingston of South Carolina Law Enforcement; Mike McKenna, investigative consultant with the Guidry Group; Jack Olsen, Edgar Award-winning true crime writer and author of St. Martin's Press's *Hastened to the Grave*, which profiles my longest running case to date; Laurel Pallock, head of the Consumer Division of the San Francisco District Attorney's office; Rick Smith, former special agent with the FBI, now president of the private investigative firm, Cannon Street; Ken Steinmetz, CHT, of Hypnosis for Health in San Francisco; Dan Vaniman, former agent with the Secret Service, now with the Federal Reserve Bank in Miami.

Table of Contents

Introduction   *1*

1 **The Con**   *4*

    Why Should a Writer Care About Confidence Schemes?; Who Falls
    for Scams?; The Big Con and the Short Con; Why the Con?;
    Criminal vs. Civil Charges

2 **Elements of the Con**   *12*

    The Pigeon Drop: A Three-Act Play; Seven Ingredients of a Con;
    Insuring the "Happy" Ending; Anatomy of a Con; The Emphasis

3 **The Ten-Step Program to Plotting a Con**   *21*

    Case in Point: Mr. K. Takes a Bride; The Ten Steps; The Dirty
    Little Secret

4 **The Players**   *28*

    The Perps; The Pigeons; The Heat

5 **Classic Street Cons**   *43*

    An Overview; The Lingo; Found Money; The Handkerchief Switch;
    Double Play; Three-Card Monte; The Block Hustle; Shortchanging

6 **Gambling Stings**   *65*

    Horse Racing; Card Games; Bar Games

7 **Carny Cons**   *71*

    The Layout; The Lingo; Three Kinds of Games; Frequently Gaffed
    Games; Beating the Heat

8 **Gypsies, Tramps and Travelers**   *85*

    The Heat; Gypsies: The Hidden Americans; European Gypsies;
    American Gypsies; Travelers

9 **Powerful Predators**   *112*

    Sweetheart Scams; Phony Psychics; Pastors of Persuasion; Grifting
    the Grieving

10 **Let the Buyer Beware**   *131*

    Direct-Mail Malfeasance; Telephone Trickery; The Classic Cons;
    Door-to-Door Duping; Retail Rip-Offs

11 **Investment Opportunists** *144*

>Pyramid Schemes; Commodity Cons; Real Estate Rip-Offs;
>Job Opportunities

12 **Biz-Op Scams** *157*

>The Players; The Deal; The Come-Ons; The Pitch; The Scams

13 **Glamour Scams** *167*

>Show Business; Publishing; Health and Beauty Bunco

14 **Genuine Impostors** *175*

>The Classics; Nigerian Letter Scam; Celebrity Cons; Copper Con;
>Various Short Cons

15 **Counterfeit and Credential Cons** *189*

>Currency; Check Kiting; Phone Fraud; Merchandise; Identity Cards;
>Identity Theft

16 **Bilking Businesses** *211*

>Telephone Fraud; Door-to-Door Duplicity; Internet Specialties; Direct-
>Mail Malfeasance; Insurance Fraud

Bibliography *227*

Index *228*

Introduction

While penning this collection of con games, I often felt like I was building the Winchester Mystery House, that San Jose monstrosity in which Mrs. Winchester continued to construct staircases to rooms she didn't have out of some ill-conceived penance for every death caused by the rifles her husband had manufactured. Although I suffer no such need for atonement like Mrs. W., I didn't want to ever be accused of not being thorough.

Trying to organize and categorize the entire labyrinth of confidence schemes initially loomed as such an overwhelming task that my editor and I decided to limit the subject in some manner. Let's stick to bunco fraud, we agreed, basically the kind of street cons associated with con artists, pigeon drops, handkerchief switches, Ponzi schemes, and the like. Out of the initial outline then dropped mail-order offers, phone slamming, consumer and business cons.

Besides rendering this a mighty short book, our plan served also to exclude about 90 percent of the confidence crimes happening today, simply because con games have evolved with our times. No more is there the same street corner society that existed before television brought our entertainment indoors. Now folks communicate via mail, phone, fax and, of late, the Internet. So how can we just dismiss the entire marketing arena when little old ladies routinely end up on "sucker lists" that magically turn their life savings into worthless junk?

And so this book is huge. And if I hadn't had a deadline, I'd probably still be writing it, because new schemes are being created even as I write this. And so in the end I declared this volume *done*, not because I'd exhausted the subject but because my deadline finally and thankfully arrived.

The Worlds of Cons

So then, how to organize these hundreds of gags into any kind of cohesive order. Should the bank examiner's scam go into "Classic Street Cons" or "Genuine Impostors" when it is clearly both? And three-card monte? It's both a gambling sting and a street swindle. And should the phony invoice scam go into the chapter entitled, "Mail-Order Malfeasance" or "Bilking Businesses"?

And then there are those hybrid scams. Con artists are forever producing their own variations on a theme, accomplishments of which I'm sure they're quite proud. I just wish they'd consider for a moment how this complicates the life of a con-game anthologist.

In the end, I came to realize that our society has many subcultures, each inhabited with its own particular brand of con games, pigeons, perps and heat. The carnival. Retail. Religion. No matter what the environment, a synergy takes place between these factions, which is perfected until a scam comes along that is so perfect that it works a good portion of the time. And so I've tried to re-create these tiny worlds, peopling them with glamour scammers, biz-op opportunists and bait-and-switchers, each weaving their own brand of larceny. Chapter by chapter, I invite you to visit life's underbelly, exploring the lingo and the mind-set that makes perps perps and pigeons pigeons.

As a California licensed private investigator, I've become familiar with most of the offenses detailed within these pages, either because of my job, my "Ask Rat Dog" column or my colleagues' sharing of their many cases.

One of my earliest concerns, and certainly the longest running to date, involved a group of Gypsies pulling sweetheart scams and caretaker cons on San Francisco's elderly. So complicated was this scheme that it took four years before it finally reached the grand jury. Arraigned on ninety-six counts ranging from conspiracy to commit murder to elder abuse, eight defendants are now awaiting trial. Their story has been told on ABC's *20/20*, in *Newsweek*'s December 1, 1997, issue and in Edgar Award-winning Jack Olsen's *Hastened to the Grave* published in 1998 by St. Martin's Press.

This graphic and gruesome saga demonstrated firsthand the betrayal victims can suffer at the hands of someone they trust. It showed me that a smart perp makes more money, safer and faster, by flapping his lips than by hitting somebody over the head with a baseball bat. And lastly it demonstrated that our fine justice system often simply ignores confidence schemes because they're just too difficult to investigate and prosecute.

O N E

THE CON

"If it looks like a duck and quacks like a duck, it's a duck."
—Old Law
Enforcement Saying

When I was a little girl, I had the notion that the entire world centered on me, a concept I still, on occasion, attempt to promote. In this fantasy, I'd determined that Earth was created solely for my benefit and that streets, houses and amusement parks were merely sets that someone went along and assembled before I arrived and tore down as I passed. Every mirror was a camera where my fellow man watched my every move, so amusing was I. These videos were then televised continually, much like the soap operas my grandma watched. The sleeping episodes, I'm sure, must have been particularly entertaining.

This theory evaporated in time, and eventually I was able to go to the bathroom without throwing a towel over the mirror. My mother in particular assured me such things just don't happen. During the middle of a hissy fit, as I recall.

Or do they?

Unbelievably, my little narcissistic world is just the sort of fantasyland created during the perpetration of a good con game. Whether the set is actually fabricated or the confellow's glibness sets the tone, the result is an altered reality in which the mark feels free to fall in with a new set of rules that he might otherwise question.

We see "legitimate" examples of this sort of sales every day. In multilevel marketing seminars, enthusiastic recruits often find themselves purchasing gallons of dishwashing detergent, convinced their neighbors will not only want to take it off their hands but anxiously join the soap crusade, as well, while across town, otherwise astute investors acquire time-share properties sight unseen and without comparing land values.

Much of what passes for business deals, telephone solicitations and mail-order offers are actually scams, carefully worded to stay just inside the law, proclaiming much but promising nothing. But in all cons, this altered reality exists, and everyone but the mark is in on the gag. Rarely does the pigeon consider the scenario was created solely for him. And why should he? Everybody knows that kind of paranoia can land you in the loony bin.

Why Should a Writer Care About Confidence Schemes?

OK, so say your thing is murder, and the genre demands a body on the floor, not a pigeon left holding a *mish roll*, that real-looking stack of phony ones. So why am I bothering you with all this? Well, because

1. Killers don't just drive over to the gun shop straight from delivering turkeys to the poor. Nope, they had a long life of dirty tricks where they've been honing their sociopathic skills with things like pigeon drops, boiler-room antics and insurance fraud.

2. A good story often demands that the perp fool the reader, which means he needs to be, almost by definition, a good con man.

3. Novels are not about folks who arbitrarily "go postal" for no good reason, but about people with motives. And what better motive than being betrayed?

Who Falls for Scams?

Quite simply, all of us fall for scams. Because as long as there is a lottery, we the people of the United States must believe in getting something for nothing. It's the law. And why shouldn't we? Because not to believe is simply not an option for anyone worth his weight in denial.

And so those who dream of stardom are especially susceptible to glamour scams. And those who fancy themselves entrepreneurs are tempted by biz-op schemes. And even the single welfare mom, who you might think has nothing to lose, has been known to invest $100 in a chain letter.

The Big Con and the Short Con

There are basically two kinds of cons, and they are defined not so much by a time limit but by whether the victim is left alone or not, or is taken for the money that he is carrying rather than sent to the bank for more.

If you intend to write about cons, it's likely your story will center on one long con with a bunch of shorties as setup. Most any short con in this book can be elongated and its components exaggerated to give it the depth and breadth necessary to turn it into a big con.

The Big Con

In the far-fetched tale of trickery, *The Sting*, Robert Redford and Paul Newman effected a big con, so defined not just because it took several days to execute, but due to the extensive fictional setup necessary for its execution. Such elaborate schemes seldom happen in today's world, but our agency witnesses big cons every day, primarily in the form of sweetheart scams. These elderly victims are fleeced for years, their assets systematically drained and their hearts resoundly broken. More often than not, the con ends only when the victim has nothing left to give.

The Short Con

Most modern schemes are deemed short cons. The old quick in-and-out is the crime of choice because

- It's simpler to pull off.
- There's less chance of getting caught.
- The victim can seldom identify the perp.
- There's less time invested should the project fail.
- It doesn't take a whiz kid to do it.

Why the Con?

Our client was considering hiring a consultant who promised to peddle their undervalued stocks to eager offshore investors. His fee was 20 percent, plus a $2,500 retainer. Our client's request was simple: Was "Jerry Lane" legit?

In short order, we discovered: Lane's address was a mail drop, and his phone was issued under another name. His references were all phony, and the companies they worked for didn't exist either. Under a list of aliases, Lane had a long list of unsatisfied clients who all reported the same thing; once the retainer was paid, Lane's job was over.

In addition, we learned the Vancouver Stock Exchange had issued a general fraud warning regarding Lane, and the Royal Canadian Mounted Police were interested in his whereabouts, as well. Suddenly our fax lines were clogged with documentation from Lane's past customers and present detractors.

One such client said Lane became abusive when he'd declined to invest. "We received your call," Lane scrawled in a note. "Since you're not faxing us back a signed agreement or paying us a retainer, you are not serious!" To someone else, he wrote, "Thank you for your letter. I'm afraid we don't understand it, however. What is the problem with our proposal?" Even as we were compiling our report, Lane continued to harass our client to send off his up-front retainer. Often and obscenely.

Obviously, our client passed, but with his permission we alerted the local FBI. The San Francisco bureau shuttled the case to Marin County, who tossed it back again. Both police forces passed, as well, declaring it a civil dispute and a small-claims one, at that. Our argument that hundreds, perhaps thousands of folks had been swindled nationwide, as well as in Canada, fell on deaf ears.

Then one cop mentioned that Jerry Lane had received some press under another aka, his true name. Given that, we accessed Lexis-Nexis's extensive news file again, this time with better luck. "Stop Me Before I Steal Again," read the headline from a 1995 magazine article.

The article quoted Jerry Lane as admitting he had conned millions of dollars from hundreds of companies over the last decade. Unable to live with his compulsion to swindle any longer, he wanted to make a clean slate of it all—with the media, with authorities, with his victims.

The mag itself declared that Lane stole "nothing to yelp about," and the scheme was "not particularly clever." In a press release to the magazine and others, Lane readily acknowledged what we already knew. That via telephone, mail and fax, he promised to bring eager, deep-pocketed investors to his clients' doorsteps, yet after receiving their up-front money, he simply did nothing. He'd fax his marks phony references and fake investors he claimed to represent. If victims checked his references, they'd reach Lane via a forwarded phone.

Claiming he decided to come clean after his young son heard him using a phony name, Lane now wanted to turn himself in—and, oh yeah, sell his story to Hollywood. He proceeded to fire off a host of press releases, figuring this would lead to well-paying talk show gigs. Then, of course, there was his book (mostly written) and screenplay (already optioned) both waiting in the wings.

Trouble was, Lane found, as we had, that he couldn't get himself arrested. And further, that an inconsequential con is basically a man without a book deal. In the end, when there proved no percentage in going straight, Lane simply went back to what he did best—perpetrating his creatively challenged scams.

A funny story. Except, of course, that Lane's victims were very real; their numbers were growing, and no law enforcement entity was the least bit interested—even after the self-proclaimed culprit had not only confessed but practically presented himself jailside, carrying the evidence in his own hip pocket.

Criminal vs. Civil Charges

OK, say your character has invested in a doughnut franchise across the street from a police station, figuring no way can he lose. The former owner tells him the cops come by daily, but doesn't mention it's because drug dealers inhabit the back booth. Your fellah gets robbed twice, and when the cops come to raid the joint, all the decent doughnut eaters beat feet.

So what is this? A mugging?

Nope. No violence.

A con?

Yep. Well, maybe not so much. Did the owner willfully, maliciously lure your character into this bad business deal or was it just a case of let the buyer beware?

Yeah? Think so?

OK, that makes it civil. So your guy sues. For fraud, since the former owner neglected to disclose the presence of drug dealers, nor did the Food and Drug Administration (FDA) designate doughnuts as their own food group as he'd intimated they would. But since fraud is by its very nature a criminal act, then why is it even possible to sue civilly for fraud, as well as embezzlement?

In the end, after many frustrating years in this work, I've decided that whether a con is considered a civil or a criminal matter has less to do with malicious intent than with the size of the district attorney's workload and his budget. No matter what the elements, take away the violence and most DAs will encourage the victim to go civil, as in go away. Why? Because they already have ten times more cases than they can handle, and this one, simply put, has not been chosen.

Determining Factors

So if a con can go either civil or criminal, what are a DAs deciding factors?

Caseload

A bad-check charge might not get a mention in the *New York Times*, but in Peculiar, Missouri, it's undoubtedly fodder for a six-week jury trial.

Dollar Amount

Most DAs have a dollar cutoff. San Francisco's, I think, is $150,000. Anything under that, and the perp skates. Think they know that? You betcha.

Number of Victims

Now, normally nobody's going to track down the perp of a $20 shortchange, but if a school of elderly keeps getting ripped off, it just might behoove the DA (especially around election time) to close down that bingo parlor.

Evidence

Remember O.J. Simpson? Discussions as to why he was deemed "guilty" in the civil trial and "not guilty" in the criminal trial will continue long after Sydney and Justin publish *their* books, but pundits agree the defining factor was the obtainable goal of "preponderance of evidence" versus the sly "guilt beyond a reasonable doubt." Since nobody thus far has explained the latter so that anyone with an IQ under 180 can understand it, a criminal conviction in America remains as elusive as product endorsement contracts for the aforementioned Simpson.

Bottom line: When the DA does not have the evidence, he simply passes on the case. Which is why you always hear them bragging about winning every case they ever prosecuted.

The Victim

Many DAs won't take sweetheart cons, for example, since it's unlikely the jury will feel sufficiently sorry for a sixty-year-old woman who was silly enough to consider that a twenty-seven-year-old Antonio Banderas look-alike really thought she was swell. Who's to say it wasn't a mutual exchange of love for money? Perhaps she's just angry that he's now moved on. OK, he used her yacht to move in, but still.

Media Attention

DAs turn down cases every day for nasty schemes that wipe out people's life savings, rob them of their dignity and future security, and leave them unsure of their own decision-making capabilities. Most times this goes down quietly, and only the victim and his friends know there'll be no justice. But then along comes a fat juicy news story, and suddenly the DA makes a giant leap into the pool of human kindness. Actually, prosecuting authorities cannot *not* be interested in the light of even the slightest media attention. What are they to say to their constituents? "Yeah, awful thing, old Doc Miller's falling for a pigeon drop, but 'scuse me, we're a little busy getting reelected around here!"

T W O

ELEMENTS OF THE CON

"All good stories must have a beginning, a middle and an end."

—My high school
English teacher

If you think of a con as a play, which it is, it's easy to see how the confellow and victim are both "actors," although the latter, of course, is completely unaware of his role in the improv. In the detective agency, we use this concept all the time. Our "con" is called the *pretext call*, and its purpose is to elicit information, usually by phone, that will allow us to continue our investigation. Using our powers for good and not for evil, the usual scenario is to confirm someone's location. The gag must be carefully thought out: If I say this, and they say that, then what do I say?

One common ploy is to ask, "Is Stephi there?" when looking for a Stephanie Burke. With a wrong number, the return volley is almost always, "Sorry, fellah, wrong number." But if we've reached the right party, most scoundrels cleverly inquire, "Stephi? Uh, um . . . who wants to know?" At that point, it's easy to back out of the conversation with,

"I'm sorry, is this the Capwell residence?" leaving no one the wiser. Had the pretext not been carefully thought out, and instead the initial question was, "Is Stephanie Burke there?" then it would have been necessary to tell Stephanie why we wanted to talk to her, perhaps blowing the entire investigation.

One inexperienced investigator tried a pretext call on *our* office, and when he didn't get the desired response (to elicit our physical address), his only rebuttal was, "Well, then, you can just die!" That, in my opinion, was not a well thought-out pretext call.

Now, like all good works of art, this "play" demands a beginning, middle and end. So the confellow carefully plots his script, taking into account that he does not have total control over the other actor and allowing for contingencies. The happy ending he seeks, of course, is the successful transference of the victim's assets into his own.

The Pigeon Drop: A Three-Act Play

ACT ONE

Late afternoon. Supermarket parking lot.

MOOCH, an old man, shuffles along, carrying his bag of oranges. CON approaches, offers to tote his heavy load and makes small talk as they progress toward MOOCH'S car.

CON
Hey, look! Somebody dropped their wallet!

MOOCH
We should turn it in to the supermarket office.

CON
Let's see if there's identification. . . . (*CON opens the wallet. Close-up of a wad of bills that would choke a dalmatian. He*

flips through and finds at least a hundred $20 bills.) There's no ID!

MOOCH

Well, the person who lost it will surely go back to the supermarket and ask.

BYSTANDER

(Approaching.) Hey, what's hanging?

CON

We found this money and don't know who it belongs to.

BYSTANDER

Let me see that. *(He takes the money from CON and examines it.)* Why, I'll bet this is drug money!

MOOCH

Why do you say that?

BYSTANDER

Look at all this cash! Nobody but drug dealers carry this much cash!

CON

Drug dealers won't go back to a grocery store and ask about their stash!

BYSTANDER

And even if they did, they don't deserve this money. It's ill-gotten gains!

MOOCH

So what do we do?

CON

I say we split it between the three of us!

MOOCH
Is that legal?

BYSTANDER
Well, friend, as it turns out, I'm an attorney, so I know about these things. The law says we must place the money in a safe-deposit box for three months. If nobody shows up by then, we can legally split the money!

MOOCH
How can we be sure one of us won't just steal it?

BYSTANDER
Do you have a safe-deposit box?

MOOCH
Yes, I do.

BYSTANDER
Well then, that's where we'll keep it! We trust you. But for all our safety in this matter, we should all put up some kind of good-faith bond—say, $150 each—to make sure none of us steals the money.

MOOCH
(Eyeing the loot.) That sounds fair.

BYSTANDER
Do you have that much on you?

MOOCH
No, I don't, but I can get it.

CON
(Pointing.) There's an ATM right over there!

BYSTANDER
Let's go!

ACT TWO

The ATM a few minutes later.

MOOCH withdraws $300 (the limit) while CON and BYSTANDER busy themselves behind him. MOOCH gives CON and BYSTANDER $150 each, and they hand over the wallet. All exchange good-byes and promise to meet back in three months.

ACT THREE
Inside the bank, the next day.

MOOCH opens his safe-deposit box and counts the money. The outside bill's a twenty, but inside it's just cut-up newspaper. Close-up of MOOCH's sad face.

Fade to black.

THE END

Seven Ingredients of a Con

So why does this classic still work almost six hundred years after its inception? Specifically, because it contains all seven ingredients necessary in a successful sting.

1. **Too good to be true.** Free money for doing nothing. What's not to like?
2. **Nothing to lose.** The old man thought he was holding the loot, so he felt in control.
3. **Out of his element.** This hasn't happened to Mooch before, so he knows no protocol and defers to the others' expertise.
4. **Limited-time offer.** Some decision has to be made by the time the three part company. There's no opportunity to consult family or friends.

5. **References.** Bystander appears as a rational third voice who just happens along. As a bonus, he's also a "legal expert."

6. **Pack mentality.** Both Con and Bystander seem in agreement on a viable course of action. Even if dubious, who is Mooch to disagree?

7. **No consequences to actions.** Since this is "drug money," nobody will report it missing and they certainly can't be accused of stealing it.

Insuring the "Happy" Ending

And so Con and Bystander just made three hundred dollars between them for ten minutes of blah-blah in a parking lot. Altogether a better living than mugging, you'd have to agree.

Will the old man report this incident to police? Not likely, since

1. To do so would be to admit he planned to keep drug money, which any honest citizen knows should have been reported to the authorities. Mooch might even be named an accomplice, thereby initiating his own criminal record at age eighty-nine. (Or so he thinks.) Furthermore, he'll undoubtedly be on probation until he's ninety-three.

2. Mooch can't identify the suspects and can't even report their names. So, even if the cops don't arrest him, they'll probably just ridicule him and he won't get his money back anyway.

3. If his family finds out how stupid he is, they'll undoubtedly put him in an old folks' home.

Anatomy of a Con

Just as successful sales techniques can be analyzed and learned, so can the components of a con. Since this is, after all, still just a transaction between two parties, the subtleties of those dynamics often determine the success of the entire exchange.

The Motivation

It can be the lure of getting rich quick, a willingness to lend a helping hand or even help in catching a thief. Whether the incentive is money, peace of mind or a warm fuzzy feeling, there simply has to be something in it for the victim or he just won't play. The incentive for Mooch, of course, was the money.

The Come-On

This is where the confellow encourages whatever the victim's incentive happens to be, assuring him there'll be no negative repercussions for his actions. He might flash some phony credentials or simply override objections with the sheer force of his personality. Here the come-on was declaring the cash "drug money," thereby insinuating nobody was ever going to claim it.

The Shill

Seemingly a stranger, this third party reinforces the victim's participation. In this case, Bystander be thy name.

The Swap

Out with the genuine, in with the gyp. Most often the switch is made during a diversionary tactic, in this instance while Mooch was busying himself at the automatic teller.

The Stress

To work, this now-or-never proposition must always be completed before someone with judgment happens by. Usually it is presented as a limited-time, one-time offer, or they might insist another taker is waiting in the wings. Here the very setting, a parking lot, demanded the deal be completed within a short span of time. Traditionally nobody spends much time in a parking lot.

The Block

The victim must be dissuaded from reporting the con to the coppers. Usually shame, embarrassment, fear, culpability or a combination of these concerns does the trick. Mooch, of course, was concerned that his advanced age would render him a candidate for the old folks' home.

The Emphasis

Since the purpose of a con is to get something from someone who wouldn't give it up if they knew everything, the con artist relies largely on smoke and mirrors to work his magic. For examples of this, we've only to explore much of the copywriting that lands, magically, in our mailboxes every day. Now, I'm not suggesting all mail-order offers are frauds, but since both cons and sales depend on persuading someone to part with their dough, sales and cons contain many common elements.

FAY FARON
IS GUARANTEED TO BE PAID THE NEW
$1,000,000.00
PRIZE!

What's not to like? A check is enclosed, and it's got my name right on it. They tell me a financial officer is standing by to help me invest my impending fortune so I will never again have to listen to some sorry pigeon relate how she spent $5,000 for tar that fell like rain from her roof. And all because I am the luckiest, most special person in the world, I know, deep down, I've only to go to my mailbox to have good things happen to me.

But wait. What's this small print right above it?

And this other stuff underneath?

Odds of winning at a random drawing are determined by total number of eligible entries received.
Distribution of printed forms is estimated not to exceed 120,000,000.

A truer representation might have read,

THINK YOU,
FAY FARON,
HAVE A SHOT OF WINNING
THIS MILLION $ PRIZE?
THINK AGAIN!
SINCE YOUR ODDS ARE ONE IN 120 MILLION,
WHY EVEN BOTHER LICKING
ALL THESE STAMPS?

Now that's clear! Instead, this copywriter chose to announce the odds in pint-size print, and even changed the form of the numbers so that the $1,000,000.00 prize ($1 million) looked bigger and the 120,000,000 (no decimal point) looked less overwhelming.

It's called emphasis. Call attention to the bounty and downplay the reality. It's what a con is all about: Show the prize, describe the prize, discuss delivery of the prize, and then mention in teensy tiny letters that the pigeon's chances of actually winning the prize are one in, roughly, none.

THE TEN-STEP PROGRAM TO PLOTTING A CON

"Who's afraid of the Big Bad Wolf?"

—Little Red Riding
Hood, before the fall

If con artists share any common trait, it's their uncanny ability to persuade a seemingly competent person to go along with their cockeyed story. To do this, they employ the same sort of psychological tricks used in high-pressure sales. And just like a good story writer, they create a sense of suspense, expectation and desire.

So how can you create this sort of fictional world where the con artist is able to lead the mark down to the cliff's precipice, encourage him to take off his shoes and fling himself into oblivion? That alone is a challenge, but consider now that your plot requires the mark not only to make the perp his beneficiary, but to stop along the way and up his insurance benefits. If you're going to attempt such a dazzling feat, best you learn from the experts.

Case in Point: Mr. K. Takes a Bride

About a week after ninety-two-year-old Mr. K.'s wife died, along came April, who was so taken by his seven-year-old

American-made auto that she felt compelled to ring his door-bell and inquire if the vehicle in the driveway was for sale.

From that initial "chance meeting," April and Mr. K. became friends. When the car wasn't exactly what she wanted, he purchased for her a brand-new Mercedes SL. When April's kiddie needed an operation, Mr. K. forked over $10,000, no questions asked. Soon, other emergencies arose, but Mr. K. was not totally susceptible to her charms. She got a lot, yet still just a fraction of the $5 million he managed as executor of the family trust.

Then one day, April arrived with Silvia, a dumpy middle-aged "widow" who was far more solicitous of Mr. K.'s cranky ways. Mr. K. fell hard for his bride, as the Gypsy soon managed to become. Silvia's "brother" carted her to and from his suburban home, yet she rarely stayed the night, except for the ones following the days his $8,000 monthly stipend routinely arrived.

Still, while she was there, Silvia must have been one heck of a wife, because soon the previously parsimonious Mr. K. was awash in generosity. Within a few months, Silvia had misappropriated his monthly income, run all his credit cards to their limit, depleted one $600,000 trust fund and was preparing to do the same with another.

To thwart this endeavor, Mr. K.'s family called our agency. Our task was to prove criminal intent on the part of Silvia. To do this, we intended to show her brother was actually her husband, married not by our court system but in a ceremony recognized by the Romany community. The new trust fund executor intended to use this proof, not for the DA, but simply to convince Mr. K. what a rotten little liar his beloved Silvia was and to get her to go away.

That did not happen. It wasn't that we couldn't get the documentation; we had a six-inch-thick evidence file linking Silvia to her "brother" and their ten children under a number of addresses and aliases. The problem was simply that Mr. K. was in love. His answer to everything was "I'll have to ask Silvia about that"! And one flash from Silvia's ample bosom sent the questions spinning right out of his head.

With Mr. K.'s access to the trust fund severed, Silvia's

visits became still scarcer. After a financial conservator was appointed, the credit cards were cut off and his income controlled, Silvia pretty much evaporated altogether. We were off the case.

The old man mourned. He sat in the all-pink interior Silvia had painted his family home and obsessed about his "young" bride who flashed her droopy bosom and lovingly brought him takeout from Burger King. Christmas came and went and still no Silvia. Finally, Mr. K.'s family was able to convince him to start divorce proceedings. Since Silvia couldn't be located, a newspaper notice served to inform her of la dump. With the disillusionment almost final, Mr. K. even prepared to marry again, this time to his deceased wife's eighty-five-year-old sister, Betty.

Then Silvia was back.

First came the phone calls. When the family spirited him off to his intended's, the willful wench found and called him there. But Betty was no match for sexy Silvia. Silvia then called Mr. K.'s live-in housekeeper and told her to "get that woman out of my house." With that, she fled, and Mr. K. left Betty, flying into the arms of his beloved.

Suddenly, we were back on the case. This time, our assignment was to watch the house from sunup to sundown, and if Silvia tried to whisk the old man away, to follow. Meanwhile, the DA was working furiously to gather enough evidence to arrest Silvia before she could take off with the old man.

I had the pleasure of being on stakeout when the authorities came to take her away. The first time I ever saw Mr. K. in person was when he tearfully watched a sheriff cuff his sweet baboo and push her head down into the car. Although I felt profoundly sorry for the lovesick old guy, I'll admit I was cheering my bloody head off.

"We're going in!" I sang to my chief investigator, Ann Flaherty, as soon as she drove up to relieve me. The conservator had called the car phone, saying she'd just talked to Mr. K. and he seemed disoriented and possibly even drugged.

The old man wasn't drugged, as far as we could tell, but he was certainly a man in love. All he could talk of was

Silvia and how he had to go pay her bail and get her out of the slammer. And he was the victim! We tried to kindly tell him what a not-nice person she was, but all he would say was that she was always good to him. The confusing paper trail of her family's akas was beyond him, and since she acquired her Gypsy husband without benefit of legal papers, we couldn't even prove she had one. Perhaps to a grand jury, but certainly not to him.

We left shaking our heads and asking ourselves what right we had to tell this old man he couldn't have his Silvia. Doesn't everybody have the right to a dysfunctional relationship? And if we felt this way, knowing all we did about this organized group of con artists, what on earth would a jury make of it?

Seventy-two hours later, Silvia was not only free, but back in the house with the victim. Twenty-four hours after that, she accomplished what we all feared; she took Mr. K. off to parts unknown.

Ann and I were livid—along with the DA, Mr. K.'s conservator and his various family members. We prepared a media blitz, officially labeling her a kidnapper and offering a reward for information leading to the elder's whereabouts. Given that Gypsies are enthusiastic snitches, we had hopes a few thousand bucks would ferret her out.

Soon Silvia was back again, asking a family member to meet them at the airport. The story was she'd taken Mr. K. to a Los Angeles attorney to inquire about her rights. The savvy solicitor, however, had taken one look at the doddering old guy and told his client she couldn't keep him. When they said good-bye at the airport, Silvia refused to give her husband her phone number, saying her attorney had advised her not to.

Still she calls occasionally, asking for money. At the time of this writing, she's not yet been arrested for this outlandish example of elder abuse.

The Ten Steps

So then, using this big con as an example, what components enabled Silvia to do what she did?

1. **Determine a suitable mark.** Before beginning the scam, the perp must find somebody with enough money to make the sting worthwhile, as well as sufficiently vulnerable to bite. Now while Mr. K., as near as we can tell, was unearthed via his wife's recently published obit, many victims are simply a case of random plucking. Everybody has something they can lose, even if it is just their credit, as with identity theft. While the traditional definition of *con* is "to swindle through gaining one's confidence," with today's technology, it's no longer necessary to actually talk to someone in order to defraud them. That makes everybody except folks who are simultaneously naked, homeless and bad credit risks potential targets.

2. **Gain the mark's confidence.** Remember April? It was her job as the setup person to gain Mr. K.'s trust, deliver his food, clean his house, run his errands and even accompany him on vacations, for which he unwittingly paid. April's actions during this time mimicked a friendship, and Mr. K. has never questioned her separate agenda.

3. **Show the mark the money.** *And here's Silvia!!!!!!!* OK, so it's not always money, but it is a prize of some sort, and in that somebody-for-everybody tradition, Silvia fit the bill. Had she arrived on her own, it might have seemed suspicious, but Silvia came with "credentials." She was a friend of April's, and April turned out to be a good egg, now didn't she, what with the errands and all.

    So why didn't April just become Mr. K.'s sweetheart? We don't really know, but it might simply have been a personality conflict between the two. Or perhaps April didn't have enough seniority or experience to be left with this prize, or perhaps she placed Mr. K. at the feet of her mother-in-law (which is exactly who Silvia was) like a cat bringing home a dead canary. What we do know is that by the time Silvia was called in, the gang knew fully the extent of Mr. K.'s wealth, and just how likely he was to give it up to the right sweetheart.

4. **Tell the tale.** Traditionally, this step involves clueing the mark in on how he can make a quick buck and then

counting on his greed to get him to bite. To that end, the confellow calls up his acting and salesmanship skills, along with any streetwise pop psychology he might have acquired. Now obviously, Mr. K. didn't expect to make any money via this romantic fling, but he certainly anticipated being compensated in another manner. On some level, yes, he knew there was an exchange of love for money, but because of his diminished capacity, elder-abuse experts would argue he didn't fully realize how much money he was losing, the consequences of his actions or, of course, that there was no love on the part of his Gypsy bride.

5. **Deliver a sample return on the investment.** This is the initial money the target is allowed to make in order to convince him this promises to be a really good investment. In a carnival, it's those first balloons the dart so deftly pops. In Mr. K.'s case, he fell in love. The perfect wife, Silvia cooked, cleaned and put out. (In actuality, she brought home a bit of takeout, hired a housekeeper and flashed a bit of floppy flesh.) Mr. K. was quite assuredly the happiest he'd been since his wife's death and, on some levels, probably a good time before.

6. **Calculate the stakes.** Here the perp determines just how much the mark is good for. Roofing scammers take a shot. Will this old woman pay $5,000 to have her rooftop sprayed with black oil, or might she go $20,000 for the same favor? Mr. K. had two $600,000 trust funds, and Silvia knew it. She certainly knew about his $8,000 monthly stipend and the exact credit limit on his charge cards. So financially attuned was this heartless witch that she'd determined exactly which days to arrive and when it was safe to leave.

7. **Put the mark on the send.** That's inside lingo for persuading the victim to go get more money. Mr. K. was put on the send again and again, and each time he came back with cars and trust funds and credit cards with their balances paid down.

8. **Pull off the sting.** This simply means taking the mark for everything he's got to give. Silvia played Mr. K. for

several years, continuing even after she was detained, because she knew that without Mr. K.'s cooperation, they'd never be able to prosecute. A really successful sting would have been to acquire everything Mr. K. owned, but Silvia had to settle for everything she could get before the conservator shut down the accounts.

9. **Blow off the mark.** In a really successful kiss-off, the mark won't even know he's been had. Although at the time of this writing Silvia continues to call, she does so only because Mr. K. does all he can to fulfill her requests. When she finally gets all she can—stopped because she's been cut off or arrested, or the money is all gone—I have no doubt Silvia's interest will wane.

10. **Keep it quiet.** Sometimes it involves paying off the cops, but most often this endeavor is aimed at convincing the mark not to go to the authorities in the first place. It could be because he doesn't consider himself a victim, or because he doesn't want to appear foolish, or because he's afraid of losing his independence, or even because he considers himself an accomplice in some manner. In this case, certainly all those things applied.

The Dirty Little Secret

You might ask, what did old Mr. K. possibly do "wrong" aside from falling in love? Unbelievably, in these elder sweetheart scams, subtle emotional blackmail occurs, not unlike what happens in cases of incest. These older gentlemen were raised in an era when sex outside of marriage was taboo, and no matter how "gone" they are, they know they are offending that lifelong ethical code when they engage in sex with their sweetie.

Yes, sex. Certainly not sex in the traditional sense, but through exhaustive research we have determined that early into these relationships, the promise of sex is introduced. The flashing and fondling creates for the victim a "dirty little secret" that almost always keeps him from telling his relatives about his new "friend," sometimes for years and often right up until the point of marriage.

F O U R

THE PLAYERS

"These were crass people. They'd sell their own mother. And if their mother was already sold, they'd go out and buy another mother and sell her at a profit."

—Testimony before a
federal grand jury,
regarding oil scams

Creating a colorful antagonist is one of the joys of writing fiction. Con artists have traditionally been portrayed as glad-handing outlaws, golden of hair, gifted of gab, throwing out lines faster than Brad Pitt in *A River Runs Through It*. And they are that. And more. It's the more that's the problem.

And then there are the victims. In mystery novels, they're usually deader than baseball in November by chapter two—which should be the end of their character development as far as I'm concerned. But unfortunately most publishers insist you dredge them up again, find out what made them perp fodder to begin with, and even more troublesome, make the reader identify with whatever caused that vulnerability.

And finally there's the heat. Generally considered the sanest of the triad, this protagonist keeps the dance in perfect tumble until he or she nabs the perp somewhere before the end of the last chapter. Detectives are individuals, of course, but there is a certain psychological makeup of one who chooses to right the many wrongs of society, just as there is a certain character type who writes about the wrongs of society—real or imagined.

For the specifics, look within each of the following chapters, as Boiler Room Bertha is a far different animal than Swoop-and-Squat Suzie. But there are some personality attributes that all perps have in common, all pigeons and, of course, those of us who affectionately refer to ourselves as the heat.

The Perps

Robin Hood robbed from the rich and gave to the poor—without even taking a proper commission. Wasn't this tighted wonder simply the epitome of the lovable outlaw? Real perps, although quite accurately portrayed as plunder lovers, stop way short of forking over the loot to folks they don't even know. If truth be known, perps much prefer pillaging from the poor—in judgment, age, spirit and good old common sense—than attempting to outsmart a worthy opponent. Of course, there's no cookie-cutter confellow profile, but whether a carny conner or a sweetheart scammer, these scoundrels all share at least some of the following personality disorders.

Antisocial Personality Disorder

Perhaps the number one definable feature of con artists is that they basically do not care about right and wrong. Not a whit. (FYI, *antisocial* is psychiatry's new term for what they earlier referred to as *sociopathic*, and before that, *psychotic*. The word *psychotic* was tarnished, they feel, by the movie *Psycho*, which left the public with the impression that everyone suffering this affliction kept their mothers in the basement long after they ceased to take food.)

Contrary to popular belief, not all antisocials are murderers. They walk amongst us, date us, roof our houses and offer us stock options. But unlike other pedestrians, boyfriends, roofers and brokers, they think no more of doing the wrong thing than doing the right thing if the mood suits them.

Other Personality Traits

So, if all con artists are antisocials, are all antisocials con artists? Since by definition they have no qualms about saying whatever will insure they end up on top of the heap, I'd think one would have to say yes. But there are other personality traits all confellows, from drag broads to check kiters, have in common, as well.

- They're career criminals who take pride in their skills. While preteen thugs often straighten out in time, con artists tend to be dedicated professionals who, if incarcerated, will use the time to study their craft at the feet of the masters. Between sentences, they're always practicing, honing the con until they've formulated an answer to every objection.

- They're a charming, attractive people. Especially to the opposite sex, and often to their own sex, as well. They have the gift of gab, which they apply to the victim, the cop, the judge and the parole officer.

- They're excellent improvisational actors. And since a con is a play, they're better rehearsed than Mary Martin when she washed her hair onstage in *South Pacific*.

- They're egotistical. Believing themselves to be the criminally elite, they love saying that prisons are filled with lesser minds. Rather than believing crime doesn't pay, they've proved it does. In fact, it pays quite well, thank you very much.

- They have an uncanny understanding of human nature. Con artists know people buy into a gag for just one reason—their own emotional satisfaction. Graham M. Mott says in his book *Scams, Swindles, and Rip-Offs*, "The more immediate the gratification, the faster the potential prospect will say yes to the offer."

Where Do They Learn These Bad Habits?

As you can see just from this book's table of contents, con games are set "plays," perpetrated by suspects all over the nation and down through the span of time. Since that very fact indicates they're in cahoots, where do antisocials learn their trade?

At Home

Just because they didn't bond with Mom and Pops doesn't mean little baby antisocials ignored their parents' teachings. According to Kate Cleary, executive director of the California Adoption Alliance, 90 percent of all serial murders are adoptees, a result of the nonbonding process missed in infancy. No, adoptive parents don't teach their kids to kill, but since murder is just at the furthest end of the spectrum of antisocial behavior, this fact demonstrates the potency of nonparental bonding on a person's psyche. But whether adopted or homegrown, one fact is certain: Dysfunction begets dysfunction.

Society

Sometimes the problem's larger than the family's values, or lack thereof. No matter how you want to make it politically correct, experts agree societies differ as to what code of ethics is acceptable in their culture. Some value honesty and integrity, and others the accumulation of wealth. As is evidenced in the chapter on Gypsies and Travelers, some cultures actively train their youngsters in scamming skills, but this certainly isn't the only culture where these vocations are taught at the family hearth. According to Leslie Kim, publisher of the *John Cooke Insurance Fraud Report*, the Nigerian culture produces an inordinate amount of criminals simply because that society measures a man's worth by his accumulated wealth rather than his integrity. Victims, they believe, become so not because they are tricked or duped but simply because they don't do their homework and therefore get screwed.

Incarceration 101

Since antisocial behavior's not the norm, one might wonder where a budding con artist goes to find a mentor. Since these unrepentant souls aren't attending twelve-step programs, one place they get together is the slammer. Rehabilitation? Who's got time for that?

The Books

There's been a lot of hoopla lately about how all kinds of information can be amassed from the Internet, and while that's true, the existence of such written materials is certainly not new. For years, publishers like Loompanics and Paladin Press have offered book-learning on subjects as perverse and perverted as burying family members in your own backyard. While the catalogs tout these offerings "for information purposes only," I'd pay good money for their mailing lists. I'm sure it would close a lot of our cases.

The Internet

It's one-stop shopping, accessible without leaving the comfort of one's own (mouse) pad.

Body Language and Facial Expressions

Psychologist Paul Ekman, author of *Telling Lies*, made an eighteen-year study of untruth-tellers and offers several telltale signs to watch for.

Facial Expressions

In a true grieving expression, the upper eyelids and inner eyebrow corners pull up. When a person expresses legitimate fear or worry, the eyebrows rise and draw together. Unless a person has a naturally crooked smile, smiling asymmetrically is a sign of lying. Ekman also points out that since true emotions change quickly, plastering any one facial expression on your character's face for longer than four seconds would give away his true feelings. Another red flag is a facial expression that is in contrast to a gesture, as outlined below. All these conditions, says Ekman, are difficult to fake.

Body Language

Ekman suggests that liars tend to control their facial muscles much better than their voices or body language, so if you want to portray that your character suddenly stops telling the truth and instead starts to lie, one way is to have him suddenly stop gesturing.

The Pigeons

Most of us pride ourselves on never being stupid enough to fall for many of the cons in this book. But the reason marks can be counted on to succumb to a certain swindle is because they have a vulnerability of some sort. The elderly—considered by most to be the perfect victim—have diminishing capacity to blame. A savvy businessman might not fall for a pigeon drop, yet could conceivably be so smitten with his child's precociousness that he trots her on down to a modeling mill. And a recent widower would obviously be susceptible to a mystic who claims to contact the dead. If you have a character who's destined to become a victim, you must first of all find that character's vulnerability.

When victims fall, so complete is the ruse, they often simply can't sort out the one nugget of truth that will enable the cop to catch the crook. Most can't verbalize the emotional path they were led down, and when they try, their stance seems naive at best, and often downright stupid. But whether the mark got taken because of his naïveté, gullibility, compassion, a misunderstanding or his willingness to help out another, it was a skillful con artist pushing just the right button that turned him into pigeon fodder.

The Number One Victim: The Elderly

Sixty percent of all fraud victims are seniors. Now this might not seem such a troubling statistic unless you note that those over sixty-five years represent only 12.5 percent of our overall population. And according to many cops who work bunco, far more worrisome is that most victims die within about eighteen months of being victimized.

Certain cons—the pigeon drop, Latin lotto, Gypsy sweetheart scams, home repairs, utility inspector cons, caretaker cons, home invasions, bail bond schemes, guaranteed prize mailers, bank examiner scams and badge scams—are targeted almost exclusively at the elderly.

Why?

Their Savings

Nest eggs derived from real estate or insurance are assets they often make the mistake of keeping liquid and at home.

They're Often Lonely and Socially Isolated

Having survived most of their peers, many elders live alone and are eager for company. Because they were raised in a far less complicated era, they do not regard overtures from strangers as suspicious.

They're Out and About During the Day

The work in their yards, shop, go to the bank. Simply put, they are accessible.

They Believe in People

In their day, a gentleman's agreement was as good as a written contract. Most older folks are genuinely eager to help and are willing prey for a "bank examiner" attempting to catch a dishonest teller, or a mother claiming her child needs to get into the home in order to use the bathroom.

Their Bodies Are Giving Out

They can't repair their own roofs any longer and some-times even need help writing checks. The con artist is ever willing to "help," and later it is that same frailty that keeps them from identifying the perps.

They Will Keep the Con Man's Secret

Because not doing so means they face consequences, as well. Many times they think, and rightly so, that if folks find out how they are "losing it," they'll end up with a conserva-tor or in an old folks' home.

Other Easy Marks

But, obviously, since seniors make up 60 percent of victims, the other 40 percent are come from somewhere else. Yes, it's true. We "young" folks have vulnerabilities, as well, and every time we venture out of our element and become dependent on another's expertise, we become susceptible to being swindled. Here are some specific personality types and the scams they fall for:

The Stand-Up Person

This is the honest individual who plays by the rules. Because he does, he very often cannot conceive of someone who doesn't. It's the couple who takes pity on the "stranded college student" who claims to need $20 for gas, the entrepre-neur who falls for the trick of ye ole policeman's ball, the housewife who dreams of a career stuffing envelopes. We call them good people, con guys call them suckers. When Anne Frank said, "In spite of everything I still believe that people are really good at heart," she hadn't yet met the Gestapo.

Most alluring scams: Shortchanging, charity scams, bait and switches, biz-op scams, identity theft.

The Get-Along Guy

This person tends to trust another's judgment over his own and kindly defers to others, especially if he considers that other person an expert. Not that this is a bad thing. Today's world is way too complicated for anyone to be expected to know everything about everything—which is exactly why we hire accountants, real estate brokers and, yes, even astrologers. When entering an unknown arena, it is always wise to consult an authority. Yet this very happenstance creates a situation where con artists who know just enough to walk the walk and talk the talk can clean up big time. Because get-along guys are courteous by nature, they've simply not learned that some people do not deserve respect, and so they don't know how to react when someone invades their space.

Most alluring scams: The Texas twist, Latin lotto, sweetheart scams, sales cons.

The New Kid on the Block

These are folks who basically don't know the score—however, that doesn't stop them from playing the game. It's the lonely widow who doesn't recognize a dating mistake when she sees one. It's the entrepreneur wanna-be who invests in pay phones when her expertise is in waitressing. It's the groom who buys an overpriced time-share for his beloved bride. In short, it's anyone whose abrupt lifestyle change has altered his sense of balance and therefore his judgment.

Most alluring scams: The block hustle, carny cons, sweetheart scams, auto and home repairs, vehicle sales, trailer sales, telemarketing schemes, direct-mail scams, biz-op cons.

The Stargazer

These people want to believe. Whether it's in the lottery, a new lover or a get-rich-quick scheme, these dreamers will get taken an almost unlimited amount of times simply because they *know* one day, one of these plans will pan out. Con artists sniff out stargazers like a dog on a gutter-snacking binge. The signs are the gleam in the eye, the brightening of the expression and the nodding of the head in the you-betcha tradition.

Most alluring scams: Chain letters, carny cons, fortune-telling, psychic hot lines, sweetheart scams, cults, sweep-stakes stings, glamour scams.

The Needy Nellie

These people *have* to believe: the landlord with an un-rentable apartment, the patient just diagnosed with cancer, the perennially dateless. All are extra vulnerable simply because they have so few options. And so they give their time, hearts and money to people that those not in desperate straits wisely shun.

Most alluring scams: Fortune-telling, sweetheart scams, auto and home repairs, TV evangelists, faith healing, cults, adoption scams, retirement and pet scams, credit repair, biz-op scams, job opportunity fraud, anything psychic.

The Wild and Crazy Guy

Some folks actually know better, but they just can't re-sist playing the game, thinking, of course, that they know the score and therefore will be the one to come out on top. Lottery contestants might be aware their odds of winning are a zillion to zip, yet "If you don't play, how you gonna win?" Besides, wild and crazies figure confellows are so danged amusing, it's worth a certain loss just for the entertainment value. Given their willingness to play, most of their adventures couldn't even be labeled "cons" except that they've been misled about the true price they will pay.

Most alluring scams: Three-card monte, street cons, shortchanging, gambling stings, carny cons, sweetheart scams, glamour scams.

The Greedy Son of a Gun

Running the gambit from wanting to get something for nothing to just being a bargain hunter, greedies become victims simply because of their search for the perfect deal. Both ends of the spectrum are considered the same by the con artist. He milks both motivations equally with the rationale, "You can't cheat an honest man."

Most alluring scams: Block hustles, street cons, Ponzi schemes, auto and home repairs, investment opportunities.

Businesses

Scammers often target businesses simply because there's money there, and confusion happens because employees don't consult with one another. In addition, since a business can't get its feelings hurt, it's far easier for antisocialites to utter the self-serving quip, "Nothing personal! Just business!" Whether the firm is a one-person operation or a biggie, con guys use this same rationale.

Most alluring scams: Shortchanging, shoplifting, store diversions, metal and tool sales, insurance fraud, machine repair, telemarketing, slamming, phony invoices, the delivery of nonordered goods.

Thoroughly Random Victims

Sometimes, stuff just happens. A pickpocket can target any woman with a purse and any man with a wallet. In the case of identity theft, a person just has to exist to be vulnerable.

Most alluring scams: Pickpocketing, shortchanging, carny cons, telemarketing schemes, direct-mail scams, 809 phone numbers, slamming, bait and switches, counterfeiting, forgery, shoulder surfing, identity theft.

Personality Traits

Of course, each of us is comprised of a little of one peculiarity blended with a bit of something else, which is what makes us individuals instead of the stereotypes you find in very bad novels and very vague astrology charts. And so just as astrologers combine signs to individualize, so can various behavioral habits combine to define an individual. Therefore, anyone who does any of the following things can become a victim.

Stereotyping

It's the mind's way of processing a lot of information quickly. If we had to sort through every bit of data before making a decision, most folks would still be going out the front door when it was time to come home for the night. So the mind says, "Oh, I get it. There's a door-to-door salesman, dressed like a street bum, who wants to sell me a brand-new TV that looks suspiciously like my next-door neighbor's. I'll bet it's stolen!"

And likewise when the mind says, "Oh, much better. Here's an Armani-suited wonder with a mahogany-paneled office on the seventy-second floor. He must be a really honest guy or he wouldn't have made all that money!" So we buy from the latter and shun the former, when the deal is, one is just a lot better con artist than the other. Go figure.

Bottom line, when someone's speech is consistent with his manner and appearance, we deem his deal "respectable," but when people are presented against type, our little suspicion police come out for a bust. But because con games are successful only when they are something other than what they seem, making decisions based on stereotypical short-cutting can turn a stand-up person into someone who wants to fall down and die.

Laziness/Expediency

In today's workaday world, people just don't have the time or inclination to check out every offer that comes their way. So busy people opt for getting their instant gratification right away before

- They run out of product!
- Or . . . The offer expires!
- Or . . . They lose the phone number!

This *I want it nowwwww!!!!!* impulse-buying syndrome simply does not allow for price comparison.

The Heat

Because our government is divided into four major jurisdictional arenas—city, county, state and national government—

so then are the law enforcement agencies who investigate and ultimately prosecute a confellow's activities. So while most confidence schemes are handled by the local police, an ambitious perp's misdeeds might be referred to the state attorney general's office or even the FBI. It should also be noted that many states have Department of Consumer Affairs offices, consisting of specialized bureaus that license and regulate contractors, auto and appliance repair persons, private eyes, etc., bringing complaints and cases to the attention of the local district attorney.

The Big Three
The Police

Big city forces often have fraud departments that deal exclusively with bunco crimes. Called everything from the colorful Swindle Section in Dallas, to fraud detail, to fencing, vice, etc., the police station is the most usual place a confidence scheme would be reported.

The District Attorney

This citywide or countywide entity either works with the police or investigates malfeasance themselves within a division called something like "special operations." Some DAs have a consumer fraud division that investigates and prosecutes unfair business practices and/or criminal cases. If a scam extends across county lines or if the victims are located in various jurisdictions, two or more DAs might work together and could even enlist the help of the state's attorney general.

The Attorney General

This state agency gets involved when the scheme involves multiple counties with multiple victims. Sometimes several states' attorneys general coprosecute a scheme that crosses state lines, such as a pyramid scam.

Specific Scams and Their Policing Agencies

As you've already seen, the lines between jurisdictions have already been blurred depending on the scope of the swindle and the location of the victims. To further confuse, many government agencies handle cons that affect their specific industry, as with the Department of Insurance. Here then, is a list of common swindles and the government agencies where they'd normally be reported.

Adoption scams: Police, district attorney (DA), attorney general

Block hustles: Police (vice or fencing)

Calling card fraud: State attorney general, Federal Communications Commission (FCC), public utility commissions, Federal Bureau of Investigation (FBI), Secret Service

Carnival cons: Police, DA, attorney general

Charities: Police, DA, attorney general

Check kiting: Police (fraud detail), FBI

Counterfeiting and forgery: Police, Secret Service, FBI

Credit repair clinics: Federal Trade Commission (FTC)

Cult kidnapping: FBI

Door-to-door repairs and sales: DA, consumer fraud division, state contractors licensing boards

Gambling stings: Police (vice detail), FBI

Gypsy and Traveler: Police

Health and beauty products: Food and Drug Administration (FDA)

Insurance fraud: Department of Insurance, FBI

Investment schemes: State attorney general, Commodity Futures Trading Commission, Securities and Exchange Commission, FBI

Land fraud: Department of Real Estate, DA, state attorney general, FBI

Mail-order fraud: Postal Inspector

Model mills: Police, DA

Phone slamming: State public utilities commission

Pyramid and Ponzi schemes: FTC, DA, FBI

Psychic healers: State medical board, DA

Retail cons such as bait and switch: DA (consumer fraud), FTC

Street cons such as pigeon drops, pickpocketing, short-changing: Police

Sweetheart scams: Police (fraud detail), civil remedies

Telemarketing scams: State attorney general, FTC, FBI
TV evangelists: FCC

Private Enterprise

With varying degrees of success and respect, private and nonprofit associations often liaison with police and DAs to curb malfeasance within their particular fields of interest. Although these entities have no authority to arrest, prosecute or flog, they can prove effective in bringing con artists to the attention of those who can, as well as encouraging the authoritative entity to take action.

Better Business Bureau

The effectiveness of the BBB differs by office. The better ones work with the local police, district attorney and media, as well as give out public alerts as to the dangers of unlicensed or unregulated businesses. But since this nonprofit agency relies on membership for funding—and because, like anyone else, they can be sued for slander—most folks do not realize just how ineffective many of their offices are. The truth is

- They have no control over a firm other than ousting them from their register.

- They cannot mediate grievances between nonmembers and their customers.

- Their policy is never to provide the public with information regarding complaints lodged against a firm.

- They consider grievances resolved "satisfactorily" if the offender merely responds in any way, shape or form to their generic letter, regardless of the consumer's satisfaction.

Civil Attorneys

Because DAs do not take all cases, one option for the disappointed pigeon is to litigate in a civil arena. The result is often an uncontested default judgment that is then impossible to collect.

Investigative Journalists

Their goal is always to get a good story, and since that requires a lot of product, they will very often bust scams that would otherwise get no attention from authorities. Many times, local stations have a consumer alert unit. There are also publications dedicated to alerting people to fraud, such as the *John Cooke Insurance Fraud Report*.

Private Investigators

Most PIs don't handle a lot of confidence swindles because there's no money in it, a notable exception being the Rat Dog Dick Detective Agency that rights wrongs just for the heck of it. When PIs do come in contact with swindles, it is because the client is willing to throw good money after bad. The result is the occasional asset location or background check.

National and Local Associations

Within many industries, active career people and retired folks with a vested interest will band together to tackle a problem that plagues their industry. These are but a few.

- The National Association of Bunco Investigators (NABI) is a law enforcement association made up of active and retired crime-fighting types who specialize in street cons, especially Gypsy and Traveler activity. They routinely share intelligence via annual conferences, a newsletter and a daily log.

- Professionals Against Confidence Crime is another law enforcement association that educates its members regarding confidence schemes, Gypsy and Traveler crime.

- National Insurance Crime Bureau (NICB) is a private corporation that provides insurance companies and law enforcement with access to skip-tracing databases.

CLASSIC STREET CONS

"There is no new thing under the sun."

Ecclesiastes 1:9

The term *bunco* was coined to describe that short, fast-moving swindle whereby the perp quickly hits on a variety of victims and is down the road and into another jurisdiction by the time the cop finishes off his jelly doughnut. Amusingly depicted in films such as *The Grifters*, *Paper Moon*, *The Sting* and *Traveller*, although the plot may be a bit more fanciful, street cons are consistently used to set up and define the character's modus operandi.

Whether your protagonist is the perp, the victim, or the suspect, the easy way out is to portray the confellow as an endearing antihero. Sadly, the truth is very different. Bunco artists invariably victimize both the very old and the very young, neither of which deserves being deprived of their life savings. If you can make your reader admire such a fellow, you're a cleverer writer than I.

To present some of the crude cons below in a way in

which the victim (and reader) will buy into the scenario, I urge you to tell the story from the point of view (POV) of the victim. As with all good riddles, by placing the emphasis on the wrong elements, you will succeed in misdirecting the reader's attention, just as the victim's attention was diverted. It is also wise to consider, of course, that certain cons will work only on a specific type of victim. A savvy business guy is unlikely to join in a game of three-card monte, but a teenager invariably will. Once.

An Overview

The term *bunco* is derived from a Spanish word referring to the banking business and once was used to define all forms of confidence schemes. Since then, con games have evolved into highly sophisticated and complex ruses, leaving the word to refer solely to cons of the street-corner variety whereby the success of the scam depends almost entirely on the victim's evolving faith and trust in the confellow.

Experienced bunco cops can cite no reliable statistics because so many confidence swindles go unreported. And those victims who do risk the embarrassment will often, for face-saving reasons, distort the facts in an attempt to appear blameless. This, of course, renders investigations and prosecutions ever the more difficult. Because identifying the perp is uncommon, confellows are rarely caught. And because there's no violence involved, tough sentencing is rare.

Bunco crimes are usually the work of a team, each member of which plays a specific role in the false reality they've created solely for the pigeon. Their parts are carefully rehearsed and have one common goal: to manipulate the mark into following a predictable pattern of behavior ending with him willingly handing over his money.

The Lingo

As you will see with many of the chapters, each con world is peppered with its own jargon—partly to confuse the fuzz, and partly because con guys just enjoy being colorful. To engrave your work with authenticity, dip your pen liberally into this pool of slang gathered by bunco cops from the scoundrels themselves.

The Confellows

Griff, Con, Player: The con artist.

Pimp, Old Man, Boss: The gang leader who directs the action and receives the proceeds.

Drag Broads: The ladies who work pigeon drops and handkerchief switches.

Drag Team: A two-person partnership working a victim.

Mack: The guy in charge of the drag teams.

Fake: A respected pro, be it participant or boss.

Front, Catch, Sounder, Steerer, Fake, Drag: The sincere-appearing suspect who initially contacts the victim.

Office: The guy who pretends to find the money.

Cap, Crisscross, Back: The second perp who takes over and concludes the con.

Renegade Ho, Outlaw Ho: A female con artist who won't share. (Ho, as in "whore.")

The Rest of Us

Pigeon, Mark, Lame, Square, John, Two Eyes, Trick: The victim.

Door Pops: A nosy neighbor.

Law, Man, Heat, Hat: The cops.

Juice, Umbrella, Trees: Police or political protection.

Shaky Mom: A little old lady who needs to be followed to the bank so she won't fall into the evil hands of concerned clerks.

Set Trick: A victim who has been set up by one of the suspects.

The Props

Pack: Money, racetrack tickets, porno pix, etc. Whatever's inside the envelope the suspect claims to have found.

Work Material: Anything needed for the con.

Mich (Mish) Roll, Bank Roll, Show Money, Boodle, Michigan Roll, Flash Roll, Nut: A stack of cut newspaper or phony bills sandwiched between genuine currency.

Live Mich: A roll of small yet genuine bills sandwiched between larger ones in order to misrepresent the amount. (Named because it originated in Michigan.)

The Hand Signals

Freeze: Hands held to the side with three fingers extended means, "Don't do anything." Four fingers extended means, "There's a cop. Go to the car." Five fingers equals, "Get me away from this victim."

Pull: Tugging on the ear or opening a purse is the signal for the second suspect to enter the game.

The Roller: Stroking the elbow signals a cop sighting.

Brush: A motion that signals the partner to call off the game permanently.

The Money

Nut: Expenses.

Jug: The bank.

Poke: The victim's assets.

Sent Certified: A certified or cashier's check sent from a victim.

End: One-third or one-half of the money or the valuables taken.

Payoff: One-third of the money supposedly found.

Offer: Silence money.

The Games

Game, Sting, Con, Caper: Confidence games.

Drag, Lame Skinny: A pigeon drop.

Long Con: Extensive scheme requiring an extended period of time and/or numerous players.

Short Con: A self-contained con game where the victim is never let out of sight, usually lasting no more than a day.

Stuff: A variation of the short con.

Double O: A scam requiring two confellows.

Single O: A con game requiring just one perp.

Jeff: A swindle designed for a man.

Jiffy: A game of trust.

Granny Game: A shtick pulled almost exclusively on elderly women.

The Prologue

In the Life: To be involved in con games or prostitution.
Hook Up: To connect with another con artist or organization.
Making Big, Proof: Proving one's reliability.
Hip: Having knowledge of the game, teaching it to another or rehearsing the script.
Down: Having knowledge of.
Stroll Sense: The ability to spot police or think on one's feet.

The Beginning

On the Stroll: Looking for a mark.
Pinned: When a victim is picked.
Sound: Feeling out the victim to determine the assets.
Hit On: Chatting up a victim, enticing him into the game.
Caught: Attempted to play.

The Middle

Pocket Sting: Playing for just the valuables the victim has on their person.
Working the Pack: Displaying a phony money roll to a victim.
Switch, Flip: Exchanging identical-looking packages without the pigeon's knowledge.
Cross: Angle used to trick.
Offing: Taking something of value such as money or jewelry.
Elevating the Mark: Building a victim's confidence and expectations.
Layover, Overnighter: Staying with a victim until the bank opens in order to keep him away from others who may detect the scheme.
Beat: Getting the money.
Being Made: Being observed.

The End

Blow Off, Forfeit: End of the game, the suspects have the money and are away from the victim.

Cut Loose: Get rid of, leave.
Final: Cutting one's partner loose.
Square Up: To quit the life.

Found Money

The props differ, as do the circumstances, but for those victims hoping to make a quick buck, the con artist has several schemes he can try. The granddaddy of them all, the pigeon drop, dates back to the fourteenth century when Chinese swindlers first switched identical-appearing packs on the street. They probably would have tried it sooner, but they had to wait for paper currency to be invented.

The Pigeon Drop

This classic is still being played on street corners, and, as of late, not just by *drag broads*, as used to be the case, but by men, as well. Victims are chosen either randomly, targeted in areas around banks or shopping centers, or set up by a knowledgeable accomplice and approached near their home.

The pigeon drop always involves at least two visible suspects, although there could be others acting as lookouts, as well as a phone person playing the boss.

To begin, the sincere-sounding *catch* engages the mark in casual conversation while the *cap* pretends to find a package nearby. (Or both can fake finding the package in the presence of the victim.)

Given the writing on the bundle is indecipherable, the mark is asked for her opinion as to what to do, with any suggestion as to alerting the police of course, immediately pooh-poohed. Together, the three look inside and find what appears to be a lot of money along with a note or paraphernalia indicating the stash has come from an illegal source.

The following is an actual pigeon drop note, confiscated by Detective Leroy Black of the Tampa Police Department. The note was addressed: "Hector Lopez, Streasse #109, Havana, Cuba."

Dear Jean,
    I am sending you twenty-eight thousand ($28,000.00). This money is in $1,000 bills. We have not paid any taxes on this money so please keep this matter a secret. Our plans are to be in New York on the twenty-eighth of October.

Amore,
Charles

Together the three conspire as to a plan of action. The cap suggests consulting her boss, lawyer, stockbroker, etc., who conveniently works nearby. She leaves, taking the pack with her. Meanwhile, the victim and the catch get to talking, and the catch confides she's carrying a lot of cash—due to an insurance settlement, or whatnot—sounding out the victim as to her worth, as well.

The cap returns the news such as

1. All three may split the money.

2. The boss has counted the loot and there was more than originally thought.

3. The boss also wants a cut.

Whatever the scenario, a split is proposed, which seems terrific from the mark's point of view since she did nothing but arrive at the "right" place at the "right" time.

Of course, there's a proviso. The boss has insisted each must demonstrate they can put up a sizable amount of cash to secure the trust of the others, or to launder the ill-gotten gains, or whatever. The catch, who's carrying all that insurance money, has no problem with this and so trots off to see the boss. Moments later, she returns with her share of the payoff. Now that the mark can see the profits, she's easily persuaded to ante up her share, as well—$5,000, $10,000, $15,000—as much as the market will bear. After all, the money's just for flashing, right?

The pigeon then allows one of her new acquaintances to take the money to the boss while she waits with the other. *Oops*, another snag, the word comes back. It seems the boss wants to see the mark in person, to sign papers or whatever. And so the mark enters the office complex while her new friends wait, but of course, she can find no such boss, no such office and often even no such floor. After a good long time of looking, she returns to find the suspects have fled.

Diamond Ring

Missy Z. Dupe is walking down the street, when suddenly she sees a diamond ring lying there at her feet. As she reaches for it, Bubba the Bum swoops in fast. Missy looks dejected, as she often does.

"Sorry, lady," says Bubba. "I got here first."

Missy takes a long look at Bubba. *Why, this scrounge of a bum just wouldn't look right in such a fine diamond ring*, thinks she.

Bubba seems to agree. "I'll bet I can pawn this thing for $25," he says.

"But it must be worth hundreds," protests Missy. "Maybe thousands."

"Well, I need the money, and I want to get rid of it fast before somebody comes looking for it."

What a bad businessperson, muses Missy. *Why, he could offer a reward and get ten times that. No wonder he's a bum on skid row.*

"Besides, I don't want to be accused of stealing it," says Bubba.

Well, that makes sense, thinks Missy. *I guess guys like him have to think of things like that.* Then Missy has a particularly fine idea. She'll offer the bum $25 and keep—or maybe sell—the ring herself. And so she does.

But more likely she doesn't, because even Missy Z. Dupe isn't that stupid. What's more usual is that Missy recalls her mama saying never to trust a skid row bum, and so she passes. So then as Missy turns to go, Bubba asks if she'll check with the pawnshop across the street as to the the ring's worth. He'd go himself, but it's one of those upscale pawn-shops and he is after all just a bum.

Why, yes, the pawnshop clerk tells her. That's a fine diamond ring, and he's personally seen the owner fork over $300 for the same sort of thing. Come back when the boss is here, and you've undoubtedly got a deal.

At this point, Missy will tell Bubba one of two things. Either that the ring's worthless but she'll give him $25 for it because she's grown sentimental about the worthless piece of junk, or that it's worth $300 like the pawnshop guy said and she wants to buy out his half. After the $150 changes hands, Bubba splits.

What's really happening? The rock's a phony, Missy's a dope, and the pawnshop guy's in on it. When she returns later, the clerk takes a closer look and says, oh no, sorry, this thing's fake. Bye-bye.

The Priceless Pooch

A guy goes into a bar with a dog. (Stop me if you've heard this one.) He asks the bartender to watch the pooch while he goes to see a man about a horse. The dog's worth big bucks, says Dog Owner, so watch him close now.

While he's gone, in comes Dog Lover who wants a pup just like the one that watered dear old dad. He'd pay most anything for a pooch like that one, he tells the bartender. Dog Lover then gives his phone number to Bartender just in case Dog Owner wants to sell.

Dog Owner comes back dejected. Seems the horse lost and now he'll be sleeping in the doghouse and sharing the pooch's Gravy Train, as well. Bartender then either tells Dog Owner about Dog Lover or offers him a pittance for the pup, knowing he can sell it to Dog Lover at a hefty profit. Dog Owner takes the money and goes away without his best friend, while Bartender greedily dials up Dog Lover.

What's really happening? Dog Lover's phone number is a phony, and the pooch came straight from Lice Town.

The Gofer Swindle

The bar's still the setting, the prop merely changes with the players. Sometimes an expensive violin is substituted for the dog, or as in the movie, *Traveller*, a family heirloom-type stickpin is lost by a well-heeled young con artist and later found by a pool-playing hustler. In this case, the gorgeous barkeep attempts to con the confellow, but succeeds only in acquiring the worthless stickpin. In this fanciful variation on a theme, the victim and con man later make whoopee in the sink, something bunco cops assure me rarely happens.

The Indian-Head Penny Scam

Here the setting is a busy bus or train terminal, the con artist a "bum" and the prop a bag of "valuable coins" marked with a phone number. When the helpful passerby dials the number for the bum, the coin's owner tells of the $1,000 reward, but the bum insists he'd rather have a quick hundred for a bottle of Night Train. The passerby makes this deal, knowing he'll collect the $1,000 later.

What's really happening? The bag's "owner" is at a pay phone just outside the snack bar, and the address given for collection doesn't exist.

The Handkerchief Switch

The second category of games comes under the umbrella not of found money but of loot belonging to someone who clearly isn't worthy of it. By thrusting a dumber-than-dirt catch man into the scenario, the victim comes to believe he'll be the one who ends up holding everybody else's money. There are many variations on the stuff game, the most popular currently being the South African handkerchief switch, which is, by the by, identical to the Jamaican Hustle below, just a change of countryman.

The Jamaican Hustle

Enter Calypso Joe who finds Patsy Pushover checking out hip huggers on Melrose Avenue. He says he's new in town and asks, "Where's the action?" She explains what Disneyland is and where to find it. Meanwhile, along comes Barry Shill who has no cute accent but who also needs directions to somewhere not nearly as exciting as Disneyland. Astutely assessing that Joe's calypso lilt pegs him as an out-of-towner, Shill suggests Joe get himself on over to Sunset Boulevard for a taste of the local ladies.

"Cool," says Joe, who prepares to leave. At the last moment, he turns around and says, "Oh, by the way, I'm carrying quite a bit of cash. Is this Sunset Boulevard a pretty safe place?" Shill and Patsy agree it isn't. Calypso Joe then pulls out a wad of bills that would clog a wood chipper and asks, "What then should I do with this?"

Shill offers to hold it for him until tomorrow. "Oh yeah, right," says Calypso Joe. "No way, you virtual stranger you, why I'd trust Patsy Pushover here before I'd trust you."

Patsy looks a bit bewildered, but then she's always worn her sweatband a bit too tight. Calypso Joe pulls out his hand-kerchief, stuffs his sizable wad of dough into it and hands it over to Patsy.

"I'm entrusting you with everything I have," cautions Calypso Joe. "You must watch over it as if it were your own."

"Sure," says Patsy, eyeing what must be about $100,000 in a thousand $100 bills.

"I'd feel better if you put your money with mine," says Calypso Joe. "That way I know you'll be extra careful, mon."

Patsy says OK and adds whatever's in her wallet to Joe's stash. This gives her a chance to see the cash close up. She resists the urge to lick it.

But when Patsy starts to put it in her purse, Shill objects. That's not safe there, he insists. A handbag is the first place purse snatchers look. Even Calypso Joe with his limited knowledge of American crime knows this. "Stuff it in your bra," Shill says.

"My bra is full," says Patsy, not immodestly.

"Then stick it in your blouse. Here, like this." Shill takes the handkerchief and shoves it into his shirt.

And so Patsy does the same. She takes the kerchief—with Calypso Joe's entire fortune and about eighty bucks of her own—and crams it into her bodice. She and Calypso Joe agree to meet the next day, and the three go their separate ways.

What's really happening? The demonstration was actually a switch with an identical package inside Shill's shirt. Patsy's own money has disappeared along with the mish roll.

Latin Charity Switch

Here the story is that the confellow must leave town in a hurry so huge he doesn't even have time to locate his deceased brother's favorite charity to which he's promised to donate the $100,000 he has, right now, on his very person. Same old demonstration of how to keep money safe inside one's breast pocket, and same old dejected mark in the end.

Latin Lotto

In this con played by Hispanics on Hispanics—usually in Spanish—an "illegal alien" approaches a countryman with a winning lottery ticket he says he can't redeem due to his immigration status. He then proposes the mark buy his winning voucher for a fraction of its worth and then claim the prize himself.

Now along comes that perennial pedestrian, Barry Shill, who happens to overhear the conversation. He'd like to take advantage of the offer himself, he states, although at the moment he is short of funds. To be on the safe side, he suggests calling up the lottery to verify the winning numbers. The mark agrees, even dialing information for himself, and hears to their delight the lottery commissioner repeat the winning numbers.

Barry Shill, unfortunately, has no money to offer the immigrant, so the mark is able to take advantage of the offer, but only if he can act quickly. The mark goes to the bank and withdraws every cent he's ever made, including—via a line of credit—some he hasn't. The exchange is made.

What's really happening? The "winning" ticket was purchased the day *after* the numbers were announced and so was eligible for the next drawing, not the last. But even the mark has to admit that involving the unsuspecting lottery verification operator was an inspired touch.

Double Play

In this case of déjà vu all over again, a second set of suspects approaches the victim of one of the above scams, alerted by the primary set of perps who assures them the pigeon is ripe for another rip-off.

Carrying some sort of police identification, these "police officers" claim to be investigating the first offense, which by now even the densest victim has to know has been a con. They have an air of authenticity about them since not only do they have details of the indignity, they have suspect photos and perhaps even an item taken during the first offense (courtesy of the suspects). These *badge scammers* will announce the perps have been arrested, yet they still need the victim's cooperation to catch their accomplices, obtain a conviction and/or get their money back. One slick trick is to insinuate the bank teller was in on it, which the victim suspected anyway, since victims commonly transfer the guilt to the last person they had contact with prior to realizing they'd been taken. Another tack is to suggest the perps have written checks on the victim's account, making it necessary for all the funds to be withdrawn immediately.

Three-Card Monte

Although obviously a gambling diversion, three-card monte is included in this chapter primarily because of the elaborate too-dumb-to-have-that-much-money prologue that is often used to tempt the victim into playing. This same pastime when performed with bottle caps and a pea is called a *cap game*, which used to be known as the *three-shell game* not so very long ago.

The Classic Version

"A little game of hanky-poo. The black for me, the red for you. Ten gets you twenty. Twenty gets you forty. Just keep your eye on the lady."

So hears the mark as he comes ambling down Melrose in search of a comic book. The crowd looks dazzled by the fast-talking cardsharp and the mark stops to watch. The con-fellow tosses cards down on a makeshift table and invites the crowd to guess which one's the queen. *Well, it don't take no genius*, thinks Mark, *since the dealer has bent the danged queen right down the middle.* After each of the player's successful guesses, Mark thinks, *I can do that.* Except he can't. When it comes his turn, he loses.

What's really happening? The winning player he observed was a shill. A little sleight of hand and a quick getaway are what make three-card monte *the* most prolific gambling con around.

The Texas Twist, Texas Tornado or Country Boy

Back in the 1960s and 1970s, so many grifters had played three-card monte in Texas bars, alleys, street corners and truck stops that virtually nobody fell for this game anymore. When truckers finally stopped participating, the grifters took to flat-out robbing them, and that led to actual arrests. Anxious to revive the good ole days when grifters got the money but not the time, they hit on the Texas Twist.

Typically played by a black and white team, the game appealed to rednecked, bigoted pigeons everywhere. Especially the greedy ones. Now, once again, clueless cops would roll their eyes and label the event a civil matter—and a sorry one at that—and tell the victim to get along, little doggie.

In fact, Detective S.M. Haines of Dallas's Swindle Squad says that most con men believe if all the evidence came out, no judge or jury would ever convict them. Very few detectives have been involved in a three-card monte trial simply because, as Haines says, "It is difficult to go beyond a mere gambling game and make a jury understand how a person can be manipulated to the point where he's under the control of a team of con men."

Roscoe Duvall

And so out of Home Depot or some similar business lined along the interstate, comes a white male in coveralls, age fifty-five to eighty, sporting a big diamond ring, a spiffy new pickup, and an aura that screams pigeon fodder. A black man approaches, very often introducing himself as Roscoe Duvall. In con man lingo, Roscoe's the *catch man, hit man, country boy* or *idiot.*

His story is consistent and predictable. Roscoe's from Tupelo, Mississippi, or some other Southern bucolic commu-

nity and is in the big city to pick up some insurance money
or whatever. Dumber than dirt, he waves around a wad of
bills, bragging that he gave a bus stop-based lady of the evening $500 to meet him later. (Actually, the money is a mish
roll, play loot, wrapped with a single hundred.) Now he's in
a fix because he has no transportation to meet his lady love,
and being illiterate and all, he can't read her address. Roscoe
brandishes the *catch card*, bearing the cutie's whereabouts
and offers the pigeon a quick $100 to take him there.

When the mark agrees, Roscoe tosses his white accomplices a hand signal to follow. Immediately, he and the pigeon
are on the interstate, as Roscoe knows any interracial pair is
cause for suspicion in the South. On the drive, Roscoe feels
out his prey. Does the mark have any money? How does he
feel about gambling? Is he showing any signs of prejudice?
Roscoe even goes so far as to emphasize how he doesn't trust
banks and used to let the boss man keep all his money because
the boss charged him only 25 percent interest. In short, he
makes himself out to be a doofus destined to be fleeced.

Suddenly, Roscoe has to go. Number one or number
two; it varies. They pull over at a fast-food joint, and upon
returning, Roscoe begins to question the mark's ability to
find the address. Suddenly, along comes the (white) *cap man*,
offering to help. The black Roscoe waves the mish roll, again
casting himself in the most despicable light possible by utter-
ing such statements as how he hasn't had sex with a white
woman since his boss's daughter turned thirteen. If all goes
as planned, the white pigeon switches his allegiance from the
stupid black Roscoe to the charming white cap man. Now the
cap man suggests a game of three-card monte, and Roscoe, of
course, is only too eager to play. Once in the victim's car,
the two suspects draw the mark into the game.

While Roscoe makes another pit stop, the cap man puts
forth his plan. They will be partners. He will flash a hand
signal that will tell the mark how to bet, and then after acquiring Roscoe's undeserved fortune, they will meet up and split
it later.

Roscoe's back, and predictably he loses. Then, after the
ante has been sufficiently upped, the mark selects the wrong

card, and boom, he loses! The cap man seethes when they both must pay off the despicable Roscoe, who wraps their money and jewelry in his bandanna with his own.

Enter the *house man*, who introduces himself as the manager of the joint in whose parking lot they've been sitting, and asks if there's a problem. He has no vested interest, he assures them, it's just his job to mediate all site disputes. The three say there's no problem, and the manager exits.

This time, the mark wins. Now for the first time ever, Roscoe starts to show some signs of intelligence. He'll pay, of course, but had he won, how does he know they both would have had the money to settle the score? After all, he's already got everything they had on them.

This discussion is designed to *put the mark on the send*, meaning he goes to the bank for more funds. (While unbeknownst to him, he is watched by a fourth suspect, the getaway driver.) With his return, one of two things will happen. Either the first two suspects will make a simple handkerchief switch, or the house man will offer to hold the loot. However it happens, Roscoe, the cap man and the house man will perform a *walk off* by exiting the rear of the fast-food joint and hopping in with the getaway driver.

The Block Hustle

Considered to be the bottom feeder of the crime chain, the block hustle is so simple that confellow trainees use it to cut their teeth. Fellow flimflammers agree anyone who can't pull this off probably isn't destined for a long and lucrative life of crime.

"Wanna buy a VCR?" Out comes the mating call of the block hustler from the back of a truck parked on a busy corner. Several boxes are open, one displaying a TV and another a VCR, both with all the bells and whistles. The prices are so outrageously low, it's obvious the merchandise must be stolen. But so what! Where else can Patsy Pushover get a brand-new TV with all the gadgets for $75, still in the box?

What's really happening? The box is full of bricks rather than home entertainment centers. When Patsy rushes back to the scene of the crime, nary a stray business card marks the spot.

Wanna Buy a Watch?

In this variation the merchandise is sold from the inside of a sport coat, and savvy scammers call, "Wanna buy a watch?" This time they really are watches, not bricks. They're just not Rolex watches, is all.

Shortchanging

There are two kinds of shortchange artists: those selling the goods, and those attempting to con those selling the goods. Prosecution of all these crimes is problematic because a simple, I-made-a-mistake defense usually does the trick. A really ambitious bunco cop might establish a pattern, sending in a couple of undercover guys to see if they get a repeat incident, but as you can imagine, most PDs have absolutely no interest in catching two-dollar crooks.

Conning the Customer

According to Lindsay E. Smith and Detective Bruce A. Walstad's *Sting Shift: The Street Smart Cop's Handbook of Cons and Swindles*, bartenders, cocktail waitresses, street vendors, carnival ticket sellers and ballpark beer vendors make up the top list of offenders. Note that three of these traditionally target a victim who may be mathematically challenged due to alcohol.

The Bartender's Rip-Off

E.Z. Marks stops off for a couple of pops after work. He's drinking, he's talking, he's making a play for Patsy Pushover, who for once isn't biting. Eventually E.Z. gives up and stumbles home to his empty bed.

The next morning he counts his cash and realizes he's forty bucks short of a paycheck. He spent forty bucks last night? How much were those grasshopper stingers he kept sending Patsy's way? Oh, well. These things happen.

Is this the perfect crime or what? Not only does E.Z. not even realize he's a victim, but had the bartender been caught red-handed, all he'd have to say was, "Sorry, pal. Here's your other buck." Who could ever prove it was intentional?

The Ticket Teller's Take It or Leave It

This con is so much a part of the carnival that many ticket booths are actually designed to accommodate it. Look for the freestanding booth with the scratched Plexiglas facade and the half-circle opening. Dad buys a ticket, three kids swathed in cotton candy nipping at his heels. From the outside, he can barely see the cashier, let alone his change. The teller pushes the bills forward, and the coins six inches behind. If Dad takes just the bills and leaves, the teller's made a bit for himself. If Dad realizes that coins should follow, it's right there waiting for him. If the teller's ever questioned, he'll just say Dad left without picking up his change.

The Vendor's Billfold

E.Z. is at the stadium and along comes the vendor laden with ballpark franks and a big wad of bills to make change. The vendor takes E.Z.'s twenty and holds it between his first two fingers, separate from the rest of the bills. He counts out the change, flips E.Z. a Polish sausage and is gone. E.Z. never bothers to count his change because he watched the vendor do it.

What's really happening? One dollar was folded end to end and so was counted twice. With a few of those double-deckers interspersed in his wad, the vendor can easily make an extra buck every third or fourth customer.

The Clerk's Sweaty Palm Holdout

The clerk counts out the coins by dropping them from his left hand into his right. Since the customer was watching, he just pockets his change and is none the wiser.

What's really happening? This sleight-of-hand technique is known in magicians' circles as *palming*. Quite simply, the clerk holds one coin back with the fleshy part of the thumb while handing the rest over to the customer.

The Cashier's Five-for-Ten Boo-Boo

Here the clerk simply gives change for a smaller denomination bill. If caught, the "mistake" will, of course, be corrected.

The Most Amusing Miscount

This con is a favorite of writers and filmmakers anxious to romanticize confellows and has made an appearance in almost every movie with a shortchanging bit in it. Here's how Ralph Mayer describes it in his booklet *Shortchanged*.

> A man and his teenage son attend a wrestling show at the carnival. The man buys two tickets costing fifty cents each. He hands the ticket seller a $20 bill. The ticket seller gives him two tickets, then picks up a handful of $1 bills and counts them into his hand, saying "Two, three, four, five, six, seven, say that's a fine-looking boy you've got with you. How old is he?" The man says, "Why, he's fourteen." The ticket seller says, "By golly, he looks like he's closer to sixteen. Yes, sir! sixteen, seventeen, eighteen, nineteen and the two tickets make twenty. Thank you."

Conning the Clerk

And then, of course, there are the cases where the customer pulls the number.

Big Bill/Little Bill

This particular scenario could conceivably be happening to me constantly, but I'd rather part with the cash than try to tax my brain sufficiently to decipher what has occurred.

Here's how it works. I think.

The customer purchases something for under a buck, paying for it with a $10 bill. The clerk makes change, starting with the coins. After the coins are dispensed, the customer starts to leave but is called back by the honest clerk. He counts out the remaining $9.

The customer apologizes for giving the clerk a ten for such a small purchase. "Can I get the ten back, and I'll give you a five and five ones?" he asks. The clerk hands over the ten, and the con gives back the $9, requesting the clerk count it. When he does, the clerk asks for another dollar, to make it ten.

Then the confellow says, "Let's see, you have $9 there, right? Let me just give you $11 more and you give me back a twenty."

And so the clerk does. And so would I.

What's really happening? Through a little fast talking, the con is using what he owes the clerk in change to exchange it for a bigger bill. In this case, he started out with $11 and ended up with $20, plus the change.

A Combo

In the film *Paper Moon*, they've come up with an interesting twist. They've combined big bill/little bill and a razzmatazz reminiscent of the most amusing miscount to come up with this early hint of things to come.

Handsome Moses (played by Ryan O'Neal) goes into the dime store with little Addie (real-life daughter, Tatum) ostensibly to get a ten-cent hair ribbon. He pays with a five. He's been flirting with the old-lady clerk, and so says

MOSES
Grandchildren? I don't believe it. Can you break a five?

CLERK
Well, you can believe it. I'm just as old as I look. Well now, here you be. (*Counting his change.*) That makes one, two, three, four, five.

MOSES
You know, this old wallet of mine's about to bust its sides. I'll give you five ones back, you give me that $5 bill. How many grandchildren you got altogether?

CLERK
Well, I got two little granddaughters, nine-year-old, a ten-year-old. Two grandsons, near sixteen. And I got a grandson, thirty-five years old!

MOSES

Oh c'mon, you're pulling my leg. Why don't you just give me a $10 bill. Here's the five, the five ones there. That way I won't be so quick to see it break apart. Six grandchildren, huh? My, my, my.

CLERK

I got a daughter fifty-one!

MOSES

Oh now, I don't mean to be handing you no line, but that's just pretty hard to believe. You got a fifty-one-year-old child?

CLERK

You can believe it, all right.

MOSES

I'm afraid I'd have to see it to believe it. Much obliged.

And off he goes, dragging little Addie, who's catching on to the con herself, having larceny in her heart as well as her genes. After he's gone, the puzzled clerk opens the cash register and muses, "It just don't seem quite right somehow." I'm sure the filmmakers did this more to alert the audience than to re-create reality, because in truth most victims would never have traced their day's off balance back to the visit from the fetching papa.

The Marked Bill

A few phony Bible sales later, Moses and Addie are at it again. By now, Addie's becoming quite the little grifter herself and so takes an active part in this one.

Here they hit a clothing store. Moses pays for a small item with a twenty (which was a whole lot more back in the 1930s) and exits.

Addie approaches the clerk and asks for a bottle of purple toilet water. She pays for it with a five, and the clerk counts out the change. Addie starts to leave but then turns back after "realizing" she got the wrong change.

"Lady, you made a mistake."

"Huh? I give you four dollars and seventy-five cents."

But Addie persists. She knows she gave the clerk a twenty because it was a birthday present from her Aunt Helen in Wichita and she wrote "Happy Birthday, Addie," on the back.

The clerk checks and insists, "I got no twenties in with no fives."

Then the manager comes by to quash the fracas, looks in the cash drawer and finds the twenty with the Happy Birthday scribble. A customer chimes in, "Give the child her $20 bill!"

In the end, Addie makes off with the $20, the change from the five and a piece of hard candy to assuage her tears. Not a bad haul for a first-timer.

What's really happening? It was Moses who gave the clerk the $20 bill with "Happy Birthday, Addie" written on the back, and the clerk wasn't the wiser. In another variation, rather than writing, the con sprays it with perfume that matches the con lady's distinct aroma.

GAMBLING STINGS

"You can't cheat an honest man."

—1939 movie
starring W.C. Fields

Some environments—poker games, pool halls, bars and race-tracks—are simply rife with rogues. Victims are chosen for their greed, and since perps know gambling entices folks who believe they can get something for nothing, this to them spells greedy. Stings can be big cons or short cons, depending on the victim's worth and how much time is justified in setting him up and roping him.

Horse Racing

Joe Davidson, Special Agent with the Organized Crime Division of the FBI, says there are traditionally two ways to fix bets. *Past-posting* means placing the bet after the race has been run. The second way is to bet both ways and then have an *inside man* remove the losing wager.

The Wire Game

The first big gambling con dates back to the late 1800s when Eastern racing results were transmitted via Western Union to horse parlors in Chicago. The problem was, there was a time gap between when the race was run in the East and when the results were announced in Chicago. During that short window of opportunity, the betting remained open.

And so it didn't take long for some wise guy to figure out how to tap into Western Union, translate the Morse code and get himself down to the horse parlor before the betting closed. As this glitch widened into a gulch, greedy bettors with no wiretapping skills began paying off translators to slip them the scores while the betting remained open.

But since these translators, if caught, could be looking at a long dark swim with the fishies, the next metamorphosis in this dance of greed was for translators to just pretend to give out the winning scores, which, as it turned out, paid the same as dispensing the genuine scores. When questioned, the translator simply blamed it on "bookmaker error." After all, it wasn't like disgruntled bettors could go to the authorities when they themselves had participated in the graft.

This wire game evolved over the years so that eventually entire *stores* or *big stores* were created just for the mark's benefit. This entirely fictional reality consisted of phony Western Union offices, pseudo horse parlors, bogus bookmakers, fake bettors, faux telegraphers, imitation translators, mock messenger boys and even counterfeit cigarette girls. For a cinematic rendition see *The Sting*, complete with placards announcing the steps in setting up and executing the swindle.

The Payoff

The next big gambling con, circa 1910, was a similar rope-the-greedy-with-bogus-tips extravaganza. It continues in some form or another on some level, even to this day.

It starts in a bar or other public meetinghouse, with a couple of guys bragging about their track winnings. The sidekick tells the winner to shut up and put away his money before some dishonest person takes advantage, but the winner just gets louder with every drink. Eventually the mark can stand it no more, and after a few polite attempts to enter the conversation, he literally butts his way in. Eventually the *roper* and the *shill* let the *live one* in on a secret. The race is fixed, and they've got the inside track.

An important component of this con is convincing the mark he's the one pursuing the opportunity. As with fishing, it's done by tossing out the bait, letting the sucker hook himself, and then reeling him in. Eventually the trout finally convinces his new pals to take him to the betting parlor. The inside man remains standoffish, reinforcing the illusion that Trout's in control. Finally he's able to wangle an introduction to the bookmaker, and when his "inside tip" pays ten-to-one, he's stream fodder for sure. What he doesn't know is that the race has already been run. After several of these "wins," Trout's feeling pretty confident about his moneymaking adventure.

He's winning. He's winning more than he makes in a month. More than he makes in a year. So when the roper puts him on the send to draw out his life's savings, Trout's out of there faster than you can say, "I prefer the stinky bait, thank you very much."

But when In Your Dreams merely places, Trout loses it all. Immediately, the pool hall is raided, everybody scrambles for light, and Trout beats feet with the best of them. Although he's lost it all, he's just happy to have escaped incarceration.

A few days later Trout ambles past the pool hall and, finding it all boarded up, again is thankful he made a clean getaway. A few days later he returns to the bar, anxious to be given a chance to win back his money, but his new pals never show. This being a really successful sting, Trout never even realizes he's been had.

Card Games

As with horse racing, card games are ripe for the rip-offable. One classic—described in the chapter entitled "Classic Street Cons"—is three-card monte, and played anywhere fools gather. But even though magicians routinely do sleight-of-hand card tricks, victims just don't get the connection.

The Drunken Mitt

A drunk goes into a bar, but he's not really a drunk, he's a con artist we'll call Barfly, pretending to be intoxicated. He's flashing a bunch of bills to prove what a big winner he is. He engages Trout in a poker game and "inadvertently" lets the mark see his very bad hand. Trout bets big, but then Barfly discards three awful cards and culls a straight flush.

What's really happening? Duh. The deck is stacked in the order the cards will be played out, taking into account discards. (When the cards are cut, a good cardsharp knows how to return them to their original order.)

The Tear Up

Once Trout's lost all his cash, his card mates agree to accept a check. After still more losing, the perp states he had no idea the stakes would get this high, so he's just going to tear up Trout's check and settle for the cash in the pot. Trout thinks that's a fine idea and even witnesses the "tear up." Yet shortly afterward, that same check clears his account. Or rather, clears out his account.

What's really happening? Trout's check was switched for one of several variously colored reasonable facsimiles, and that one is ripped into pieces.

The Shark

Two guys are playing a friendly game of pool, and one of them is Trout, who's winning. Along comes Barry Shill who tells Trout about this really rich, respectable citizen who *loooves* to gamble but unfortunately isn't very good at it. After much prodding, Barry agrees to set up a game in a hotel room. Trout loses, natch, and there's a big brouhaha when Barry accuses the respectable guy of cheating. The "hotel owner" shows up and says everybody's got to leave *right now* or he's gonna call the cops. Somewhere in the shuffle, Trout's winnings disappear, as does Barry, the hotel manager and the respectable citizen.

What's really happening? Wake up, Trout! They're *all* in on it!

Bar Games

Whenever anyone puts booze in his face, judgment gets impaired. And whenever this fuzziness rules, there often happens along someone who uses his own self-control to advantage. Here are but a few of the ways folks lose money in bars. For more, see "Shortchanging" in the chapter entitled "Classic Street Cons."

Put and Take

A guy goes into a bar with a little spinning gizmo and plays penny ante with the bartender—who loses. Not to worry, says Guy Juan, I was cheating. He shows how the spindle works and even gives the bartender his money back, since it was all just in good fun. The bartender's so impressed that he buys the spinning gizmo from the stranger. Exit Guy Juan.

The bartender loves his spinning gizmo since he routinely makes a buck or two off his regulars. Enter Guy Two, a fellow who just hates losing. He plays the gizmo game, continually upping the ante. When the stakes are Rocky Mountain high, Guy Two finally wins.

What's really happening? Guy Juan and Guy Two are in cahoots. When the barkeep goes off to fill a drink order, Guy Two switches the barkeep's spinning top with his own, which is gaffed in the other direction.

The Smack

A naive out-of-towner goes into a bar and sits down beside another "tourist." After a little good-natured bonding, Barfly enters and insists on buying the two a round. Sure, he's a bore and a drunkard and meaner than he is blitzed, but a drink's a drink, says affable Tourist to Naive Out-of-towner.

After a tall cool one, Barfly suggests they match coins to see who gets the next round. Odd coin buys. When Barfly goes to the can, Tourist suggests a scheme whereby they take Barfly up on his bet, with one always guessing heads and the other tails. This way, one will always win. They will split the profit afterward.

Despite Barfly's perennial losing streak, he keeps smacking coins on the back of his hand, hence "The Smack."

"One last round!" he sings. "Winner takes all!" And as according to plan, Naive Out-of-towner and Barfly match, with Tourist winning the pot.

Soon afterward, Tourist must bid adieu. Naive Out-of-towner, eager to get his money back, along with his share of the winnings, says farewell, as well. Outside, while dividing the pot, Barfly stumbles out and, spotting the split, calls them a couple of professional con artists! (I cleaned up his language some.) He's loud, obnoxious, and threatens to call the cops.

Now as we well know, nobody likes cops much when they're heading off in their BMWs after a big Red Hooks. So Tourist and Naive Out-of-towner try to convince Barfly they've never met before. Barfly insists the only way he'll buy that is if they head off in opposite directions. OK, sure, the two agree, with a wink and a nod. Except, of course, Tourist doesn't double back to link up with Naive Out-of-towner.

What's really happening? Naive Out-of-towner was just confused as to which of the three were partners.

CARNY CONS

"Never give a sucker an even break."
—Edward Albee

Your setting is a carnival. You've got your girlie shows, your freak shows, the arcade and, of course, the fried zucchini on a stick. Nothing bespeaks ambience like the sights, sounds and smells of a traveling sideshow, the grittier the better. Maybe your hero's there because he's searching for a ten-year-old who ran away to join the show, not realizing he was two heads short of the three-headed boy requirement. Maybe the character's pop is a carny, or maybe he's just convinced Indian fry bread is a food group. Why ever he's come to the carnival, if you intend to write about this underbelly of entertainment, there's a lot to absorb, most of it not readily accessible to outsiders, as they refer to the rest of us.

As you read this chapter, pay attention to carny jargon, defined below in "The Lingo." (Just perusing that section will give you an idea of how carnies view the world.) I tried to work them into the text whenever possible so you'll know I'm not just *lot lice* who's *not with it*.

The Layout

One of the first things to know about a carnival is that there's nothing there that isn't minutely planned—starting with how the whole thing is laid out. If you thought Las Vegas was the greediest place on Earth, you haven't been to a midway lately.

The Front End

The entrance. Flash is its middle name, attracting customers with its gaudy concessions, stomach-churning rides and, of course, tooth-decaying food booths.

The Right Side

The first stop after the front end. Years ago, some smart carny figured out that since Americans drive on the right and walk on the right, they would also meander down the right side of the midway first, losing all their money there first. And because he (or she) was correct, game agents on the right side not only get first crack at the suckers, they also pay more rent for the privilege.

The Midway

The physical center of the action. This is the home of the *four-way joints*, so named because they can be accessed from all four sides.

The Back End

The final point before patrons turn around and start working their way back toward where their cars have been broken into. Here you find the really special attractions like freak and girlie shows, along with the biggest and scariest rides and the toughest games of skill. It's the adult area.

The Left Side

The way back, just after the back end where the patron threw his very last dime into a ceramic dish. As with the right side, the game booths in this area are open on just one side, with their rears up against the fence. Because they are in a line, they're known as *line joints*.

The Lingo

Those crazy carnies. Like any tight-knit subculture, they create their own shorthand and speak a lingo all their own. To paint your carnival backdrop with the proper grit and jargon, you'll need to toss in some words for authenticity.

The Business

Church Call: A preopening briefing where jobs are assigned and rules explained.
Jump: A move between towns.
Location: The space given to erect a game, show or ride.
Lot: The grounds.
Play: The engagement of the carnival.
Ragbag: A run-down show.
Rehash: Reselling used tickets.
Route: The towns to be visited.
Sunday School Show: An honest carnival.
Teardown: The dismantling of a show.

The Carnies

Advance Man: The guy who travels ahead and takes care of licenses, permits, grounds, advertising, publicity, etc. He may also grease the pocket of a local official.
Agent: A game operator.
Bag Man, Fixer or Iceman: Carnival rep who picks up the money and makes the payoff when there's a beef.
Belly Stick or Shill: Someone who pretends to be a winning customer but is actually part of the show. (See "Belly Joint.")
Flatty, Thief or Grifter: Operator of a crooked game.
Forty Miler: A carny who won't travel over one hundred miles from home.
Geek: The wild man in a show.
Inside Man: A game operator who works with a shill.
Insider, Carny or With It: With the carnival.
Mender, Patch or Patchman: The carny "lawyer" who takes care of beefs and bribes.
Outside Man, Stick or Shill: A pretend customer who works

with an inside man, winning and secretly returning prizes.

Ride Jockey: The equipment guy.

Talker: The barker outside an attraction.

The Customers

Beef: A complainer.

Live One: A guy with money.

Lot Lice: People who walk around all day without spending any money.

Mark or Sucker: Anybody who goes for a rigged game. (The name *mark* comes from early carny history when an agent would actually mark the back of a sucker's shirt so his carny cronies would be sure not to miss him.)

Tip: The crowd around a game.

The Games, General Terms

Add-up Joint or Count Store: A game requiring a certain number of points to win.

Booth: A game run by an outsider like the Jaycees.

Digger: A coin-operated crane game.

Hanky-Panky: A kid's game, fish pond, coin toss, etc. Also an honest game, but one where the prizes are worth far less than the cost to play.

Joint, Store: All carny-run games, crooked or honest.

Laydown: The counter where players place their bets.

Money Store: A game that pays out cash instead of prizes.

PC or Percentage Game: The odds are with the house.

Skill or Science: A game requiring skill to play.

Three- or Four-Way Joints: Games that can be played from three or four sides.

Two-Way Joint: A game that can be operated either straight or gaffed.

Gaffed Games

Alibi Store: A game where there's no chance of winning. So named because the *alibi agent* gives advice as to why the player is losing.

Belly Joint: Named because the agent leans his stomach up against a mechanical device to control the game.

Flat or Flat Joint: So called because the player flat-out loses.

G-Wheel or G-Joint: A gaffed wheel or spindle joint.

Grind Store: A game where the player just keeps missing. So named because the agent grinds away at his money.

Peek Store: A gaffed game where the operator peeks at a number or obscures part of it.

Razzle Game: Here a conversion chart determines the score and allows the agent to easily miscount.

The Money

Break the Ice: First money of the day.

Cut-Ins: The electrical charge paid to the show owner.

Double: Twenty bucks.

Fin: Five bucks.

Fix, Patch, Ice or Juice: Bribe paid to a local official to run an illegal gambling or girlie show or to end a beef.

Nut: The rent on a game space or other opening expenses.

Oats: Money grafted before the day's proceeds are counted.

Points: The 10 percent the game operator pays to the carnival owner.

Privilege: The rent on a concession.

Sawbuck: Ten bucks.

Score: When an agent wins over $100.

Sting: Same thing, but around $20.

The Prizes

Flash or Piece: Expensive prizes used to attract customers.

Plaster: Ceramic or plaster of paris prize.

Plush: Stuffed animal.

Slum: The cheap ones.

Stock: Prizes in general.

The Rigging

Burn the Lot: To cheat the customers so thoroughly that it makes it impossible for another carnival to play the town.

Cop: To win, steal or cheat.

Fairback or Throw a Cop: When the agent cheats in favor of a customer as an enticement to up the ante.

Gaff: To control a game.
Gaff, G or Gimmick: A device used to control a game.

The Problems

Cop, Beef, Heat or Hey Rube: a complaint or minor fight.
Blank: No business.
Blow or Go Wrong: To give out a prize.

The Other Attractions

Bally: A free preview designed to entice the crowd into buy-
   ing a ticket to a show.
Cookhouse: Where the show folks eat.
Concessions: All food, game and direct-sales booths.
Grind Show: One that continues throughout the day.
Ten in One: A freak or magic show with ten attractions.

Three Kinds of Games

And they are: games of skill or science, games of chance,
and what is called a *flat game*, as in the agent flat-out robs
you. For all joints, victims of choice are the very gullible and
the very hopeful, for example, teenage boys on first dates
with teenage girls, and middle-aged men on first dates with
teenage girls.

   And the problems with prosecution? The victim, first
of all. Nine times out of ten, the loser blames himself—unless
he's a sociopath, in which case, he's so known for blaming
others that no one pays him any homage anyway. And many
times, if and when a customer does complain, the fixer simply
greases a palm or two and makes the beef go away.

Games of Skill or Science
   In a thoroughly honest store, solely by his own ability,
a live one is able to win big plush prizes or little dainty dishes.
Most games of skill can be played either straight or gaffed.
Games of science are the only legal ones of the three.

Games of Chance
   Since gambling is taboo outside Atlantic City, Indian
reservations, riverboats, bingo parlors and the entire state of

Nevada, true games of chance are unwelcome in most towns the carnival will roll through. Therefore, most games contain a skill component, qualifying them as a game of science. The irony is that although games of skill can be gaffed, their illegal sidekick, games of chance, can't.

Flat Games

If advertised under banners reading, "C'mon in! We'll flat-out rob you!!!!" these obviously would attract few customers. Therefore they also are disguised as games of skill. But they're not. It would take the gravity- and physics-defying dexterity of Superman to win a stick of bubble gum at one of these.

Frequently Gaffed Games

Carnivals may be as American as apple pie, but they can be just as bad for you. Yeah, we all suspect the games are rigged, but to say so merely labels one as a panda-less loser. And after all, if the booths were all that crooked, wouldn't your bucolic little town just kick that traveling show's butt from here to Peoria?

Now I'm not saying all midway games are fixed, but a large number are so easy to gaff that unless the game operator is first cousin to Mother Teresa, he probably can't resist tipping the odds a bit in his favor. Always gaffed games? That darn wheel of misfortune, and *count* or *grind* stores, where points must be accumulated to win. An important part of gaffing any game is in the buildup or *fairback*, the time where the agent gains the mark's confidence by throwing the contest his way. This is done to impress and entice the crowd or *tip*, and/or to up the player's ante.

Keep in mind also that individual carnivals call these same games anything they like. The names I've used here are the most common usage by cops who work bunco.

Balloon Darts

Big board. Balloons all over it. Behind them are S, M and L tags signifying the prize size that comes with the bursting. The point is to accumulate points, making it a grind game. What's really happening? Anyone can see there are far more S tags than Ms, and more Ms than Ls. What one might not realize is that some balloons are under-inflated, thereby rendering them not just smaller targets but too rubbery to take a bullet. A variation on this game, Dart Toss, is the same thing but the target is a colored circle or whatnot. In this *peep* store, the operator turns over a bull's-eye and tells you about your itsy-bitsy prize. No matter what you won.

Basketball

The hoop's just four feet away, so the star player at HoopThrower High thinks this one's a cinch. What's really happening? Even if he scores every time, he'll still spend $8 to win a $2 prize. What's more, the ball may be overinflated to give it more bounce, and the hoop might actually be smaller than the ball, obstructed in some manner or not securely fastened to the backboard.

Bottle Stand

The object is to stand a horizontal bottle upright with a two-pronged fork, ten times in a row. The game operator keeps score with pennies on the counter. What's really happening? Each bottle has a heavy side. If it's on the bottom, the bottle will stand up; if on top, the same maneuver will cause the bottle to tip over. Every time the player succeeds, the operator uses the bottle itself to push a penny off the platform. As he does so, he twists it around, controlling the game.

Bottle Ring

The object is to toss a ring over a pop bottle. What's really happening? The ring is smaller than the top of the bottle. Or there's a dried bit of clear glue keeping the ring from passing over.

Bowling Ball Roll

A coin-operated grind game where the player has only to roll the ball down a track, making sure it stays in a valley. What's really happening? The agent controls the game by tilting the adjustable table legs.

Bucket Store

Three wooden pails are placed on an angle, facing the player. The object is to toss two consecutive baseballs into them and get them to stay. What's really happening? The buckets have a secret second bottom. When elevated by a foot lever, they mesh together creating a drum effect that bounces the ball right out of the midway. During the fairback, the *flatty* demonstrates from his position at the side of the booth. From this angle and with the second bottom down, it don't take no Magic Johnson.

Bulldozer

The most popular device at the midway is the enclosed machine with the steady arm-sweep that, prompted by the player's quarter, pushes a whole slew of others off the ledge and into the player's waiting palm. What's really happening? The raised lip creates a piling effect and the appearance of immediate droppage. Instead, the equipment's designed to elbow the coins out to the side where they drop into hidden chutes and are returned to the house. In some machines, prizes sit on top of the coins, emphasizing this effect.

Cat Rack

Three shelves are lined ear-to-cute-little-ear with stuffed cats. The player's objective is to knock them over with a baseball. What's really happening? Considering the kitties are actually itsy-bitsy and mostly fur, soaring to the moon on your Radio Flyer would be easier. To further gaff, the *alibi agent* may activate a hidden device designed to keep the cats from falling. Or the device may temporarily widen the shelf, making them tough to tumble. Or perhaps it could be the fact that they weigh more than Fluffy after ten consecutive cans of Whiskas.

Cork Gallery

In this one, multicolored ten-ounce cups sit along a row of shelves waiting to be shot down with a cork gun. Their bottoms are marked with S, M or L, indicating the prize size. What's really happening? The dropped cups fall behind a board and always come back reincarnated as an S. If the game's ever busted, it looks legit because there are actually plenty of L and M cups on the shelf.

Coke Roll

The object is to mow two Coke bottles down with a softball. What's really happening? The softball is lighter than regulation, and the game operator sets one bottle slightly back so the first absorbs the strike and the second stays up. During the player's free throw, the bottles are placed side by side, so both equally absorb the energy and tumble.

Bottle Roll

In a game similar to Coke Roll, a second softball is placed directly in front of the bottles. During the fairback, the ball touches both evenly, and so they go. When the game's for real, one bottle is set back slightly, insuring the player loses.

English Pool

In this one, there's a circle drawn around a pool ball, and on the ball sits a coin. The object is to pitch a second ball in order to hurl both the ball and the coin outside the circle. What's really happening? The balls are of different weights. When the heavier ball is thrown, it will dislodge the lighter one. When the lighter ball is hurled, it just can't do the job. Or the coin might be gaffed. If the coin is dead-center on the ball, it will drop straight down, staying inside the circle. If off-center, it will be pitched. Or the agent can wax one side of the coin. Wax side down means it will stick and travel with the ball. Wax side up means it drops straight down.

Flukey Ball

This game consists of a backdrop with a garbage pail underneath. The object is to toss a plastic ball and have it stay in the bucket. What's really happening? During the free throw, the player is given a cut ball, which has less bounce and so falls easily into the pail. But in the real game, an uncut ball is substituted, for which the term *bouncy-ball* was coined.

G-Wheels or Spindles

This is that big wheel-of-fortune-like gizmo where the player wins whatever prize is indicated when the needle comes to rest on a peg. What's really happening? The agent controls the game via a hidden button that insures the needle never comes to rest on the big prizes.

Milk Bottles

In this one, one milk bottle is set atop two others. To win, the player has merely to knock them all down with a baseball. What's really happening? When one bottom bottle is placed back an inch or so from the other, it makes a direct hit impossible. To insure this outcome, the agent may also use two bottles weighing three pounds each, and one—the bottom guy, set slightly back—a ten-pounder.

Milk Cans

Some carnivals are very into dairy products. Maybe it's all that traversing the Midwest. Regardless, in this game the object is simply to toss a softball into a milk can, a task worthy of any baseball-playing farm kid. What's really happening? Not all milk cans are created equal. In a gaffed game, the opening will be roughly the same as the softball's diameter. And those low-hanging prizes don't help, either.

Nail Joint

Attracting the do-it-yourself show-offs, the object in this *alibi store* is to drive a nail into a board with just one slam of the hammer. What's really happening? The agent carries two sets of nails. The hard ones he uses for demonstration. And the soft, malleable ones, he gives to the player.

Peach Basket

Here's another one of those leftover wholesome-food-container alibi booths. In this one, several baskets are attached to an angled platform yawning open before the mark. Again, the player has simply to toss a softball and get it to stay in the basket. What's really happening? During the free demo, the agent leaves a softball in the basket, which absorbs the shock. But when the game's for real, out comes the softball (the rules, you know), which renders the basket

far bouncier. Also, the basket's angle, as well as the hardness
of the ball, determines how rigged the game is. Variations on
this game include Huckly Buck (same game but baseballs in
wooden kegs) and Pop It In (object is to toss a baseball into
a compartmentalized box).

Screw Ball

Three pool balls stand in a triangle around a golf tee—
one in front, two behind, all touching. The player is to hit
the grouping with a cue ball and knock over the golf tee.
What's really happening? During the fairback, the tee is
touching the front ball and so, when struck, it goes down.
During a gaffed game, the tee touches the rear balls. Now,
when the front ball's hit, the back balls separate, leaving the
tee clear and standing.

Shooting Gallery

Here you've got your BB gun or cork-gun Uzi, with
which the player attempts to shoot clean through a red star
on a paper target. What's really happening? Most losers think
the sight is off, and while that may be true, the alibi agent
also uses an easily shredding paper so the red star will never
cleanly disappear.

Skill Crane

There's a machine full of goodies and all you gotta do
is position the crane directly over your coveted trophy and
then push the stop button. The machine does the rest, pinch-
ing the prize and dropping it onto the exit chute. What's really
happening? The crane doesn't stop where you tell it to. Or
the chosen prize is too heavy to pluck. Or is placed at an
impossible angle. Or is sitting on a shag carpet that renders
it unliftable.

Spot the Spot

A grind game where the player attempts to cover a dot
by dropping five disks onto a playing table from a few inches
above. What's really happening? The disks aren't big
enough—except, of course, for the one the agent uses during
the demonstration.

Swinger Ball

In this alibi game, the player swings a hanging ball past a bowling pin, attempting to make it topple on the return trip. What's really happening? The chain's positioned directly over the pin, which means if it misses it going, it's going to miss it coming back. To demonstrate, the operator will put the bowling pin off-center, placing it in the ball's return flight path. Or the agent quickly pushes the ball past the pin, releasing it on the backside, something—because of the rules—the mark can't do. Or the bowling pin is stuck on a retractable nail, enabling it to come up or stay down, depending on whether it's fairback or real time.

Three-Pin Bowling

In this grind game, three bowling pins are set in a horizontal line. The object is to knock them over with a wooden ball. What's really happening? Together the three pins are so vast that when placed side by side, the ball can't possibly hit all three at once. During the fairback, the agent places the center pin slightly back, thereby bringing the outside pins closer together.

Tip the Cup

Here the object is to shoot down a pyramid of three plastic cups using a foam-ball gun. What's really happening? The plastic platform causes the cups to slide rather than topple. Setting one a tad back doesn't help, either. Another gaffing maneuver is to misload the gun, causing the ball to wobble when shot.

Watch à la Blocks

The object here is to simply toss a wooden ring over a block of wood. The bigger the block, the more expensive the prize attached; for example, a watch—thus, the name. What's really happening? W.C. Evans & Company described this in their 1918-1919 catalog as "the only safe method of using valuable watches on a hoopla stand." Sound slightly rigged? So what's happening? The larger blocks either are just barely bigger than the hoop or are slanted on top so the only way to ring one would be from behind. Where the carny is and the player isn't.

Beating the Heat

The old expression "running away to join the carnival" has some history behind it. A good percentage of carnival workers are wanted for one thing or another, and I'm not talking the Nobel Peace Prize. Many use aliases because they're on the lam.

In their book *Sting Shift*, Detective Bruce Walstad and Lindsay E. Smith say that, generally speaking:

- At least 25 percent of all midway games are rigged.
- Manufacturers actually sell crooked games or, at the very least, games that can be easily gaffed.
- The closer a carnival is to home base, the more honest the games.
- The integrity of the owner is the most important factor in the honesty of the carnival.

For cops patrolling carnivals, they suggest:

- Check all health, building and electrical permits for code violations.
- Talk to the show owner, using his own lingo, and let him know you understand how games are gaffed and that plainclothesmen will be watching.
- Ask if they want to hire off-duty cops for security, and observe the reaction.

E I G H T

GYPSIES, TRAMPS AND TRAVELERS

"The gullible are meant to be gulled."

—Old Traveler
Saying

Gypsies and Travelers. These two cultures are very different from each other, yet the Romany, Rom or just plain Gypsies and their more fair-haired and fair-skinned counterparts, the Irish, Scottish and English Travelers, both depend on confidence crimes to fuel their economy. Both groups have their own language: Romany for the Gypsies, and Cant—a mixture of English and Gaelic—for the Travelers. Both are patriarchal societies whose members have limited or no education. Traditionally, members of each of these distinct subcultures socialize and marry only within their own communities, and do so at an early age in dowry-driven unions. Both groups spend "their" money on horse racing and gambling.

Unlike the Rom, the Travelers have been, albeit infrequently, penetrated by outsiders. Because of this, more is known about them, and home videos of some of their secret rituals have even ended up on programs like NBC's *Dateline*.

As for victims, both groups identify elderly homeowners by their old-fashioned venetian blinds, lace curtains, and telltale bumper stickers like, "My grandkid is an honor student."

So are all Gypsies and Travelers tramps and thieves? To a man, cops who work this detail will, out of earshot of the media, say . . . yes. Sergeant Roy House of the Houston PD (retired) says of the hundreds he has met, "There are none whose families have not engaged in scams in the past." If you write about cops who work Gypsy and Traveler crimes and portray them as honestly believing there are "good" Gypsies and "bad" Gypsies, you're going to be dealing with a serious authenticity issue.

The Heat

This is a good time to introduce the National Association of Bunco Investigators, since there is no way to talk about Gypsies without quoting the expertise of these investigators. NABI is a nonprofit organization made up of some seven hundred active and retired cops, as well as others who deal with Gypsy, Traveler and confidence schemes on a daily basis. Between annual conferences, they exchange intelligence via a bulletin and log, alerting members to sightings of known suspects.

Another group, Professionals Against Confidence Crime, is also active in this area, and is the source for much of the info in the chapter called "Carny Cons." This group is based in Chicago.

Gypsies: The Hidden Americans

Unbelievably, most Americans aren't even aware we have a Gypsy population, because the Gypsies so infrequently roast pigs at campgrounds and keep everyone up all night with their tambourine banging. Victims describe perps as being Greek, Hispanic, even Indian, a phenomenon that dates back centuries.

How many Gypsies are there in America? Since the Rom rarely identify themselves as such, nobody really knows. Estimates of 1.5 million have been bantered about, but Sergeant House makes a convincing case of there being a mere 100,000, which he gets by extrapolating the 1,500 to 2,500 he knows to reside among Houston's population of five million people out to the rest of the U.S. population.

Bunco cops separate Gypsy crime into two categories, definable by immigration patterns and modus operandi (MO). The more newly arrived European Gypsies wear the traditional long skirts and garb associated with their Old World relatives, while the American Gypsies dress more modern, further trading tents for flats and roasted-pig soirees for IHOP's International Passport Breakfast.

The Lingo

The official language is called Romano Swato, while the lower-caste Gypsies speak Romany. To explore some of the words picked up by law enforcement is to catch a glimpse of the culture.

The Social Structure

In a Rom (Gypsy) *familya*, every man, woman and child contributes financially, with duties delegated by sex. Arranged marriages happen by age fifteen, the *bori* (daughter-in-law) purchased from another *familya* based on her estimated earning potential. The going price, about $16,000, is worth it since she will become the main breadwinner, living with her in-laws until she has children of her own.

The *baro* is the leader of the *familya*, who may or may not have their own *officia* (fortune-telling parlor.) The *kumpania* is the term for the various *familyas* who work an area and control the economic territories. The *rom baro*, or big man, presides over the *kumpania*. He's usually the richest, most robust, loudest and most aggressive—traits much admired by Gypsies. Traditionally, he arranges marriages, divorces and feasts, settles quarrels and negotiates with law enforcement. He remains leader as long as the *kumpania* accepts his authority. The best *rom baros* have a "cop in the pocket" who will, for a fee, make unpleasantness go quietly away.

The *vitsa* is a tribe of several *kumpania* banded together under a particular *rom baro*. When he dies, Gypsies from all over the country gather to pay homage, an occurrence interpreted by the *gadje* (non-Gypsies) as the death of the king of the Gypsies, which amuses the Rom greatly, given there are no hereditary kings and never have been. The *natsia* is the Rom nation made up of the Machawaya, Kalderasha, Churura and Lowara tribes.

The Justice System

A *kris* is a Gypsy court that settles disputes when the *baros* have failed or when a moral code is broken. Since Gypsies have no use for American justice, except for its harassment value, the *kris* is the law of the land. *Romaniya* is the moral code that forbids any interaction with non-Gypsies, except for the purpose of extracting money. The fine paid to an offended Gypsy is called a *globa*, and *marime* is defilement and cause for exile from the community.

The Rest of Us

Gadji, *Gadjo*, and *Gadji*, are non-Gypsies—female, male and both, in that order. Another term for outsiders is *marimos*, coming from the word *marime*, as in *unclean*. The *jawndari Rom* is the "Gypsy cop," meaning a police officer hip to their ways. The *baro ri*, is the big cop, that is, his boss.

The History

A Gypsy once told me he asked his grandmother from where their people had come, to which she'd replied, "The Old Country." Which old country she could never say, because the family had no use for boundaries and, being illiterate, didn't pay much attention to the road signs, either.

Since the Romany language is historically an unwritten one, it's difficult to definitively reconstruct this people's history, but their touchstone legend dates back to 0 B.C. and is a tale that, ironically, explains why Gypsies steal. As the story goes, a Gypsy blacksmith was summoned to make four nails for Christ's crucifixion. When the tooler awoke a day later, he found one nail glowing. Before he could even gulp down his morning coffee, along came an angel who explained that the spike was meant to be driven through the heart of Jesus and so instructed him to steal it, thus saving Jesus this additional agony. As a result of this kind act, God decreed the entire clan could wander the earth, stealing whatever they liked. Several versions of this tale exist—the blacksmith eats the nail, a small boy makes off with it, etc.—but the punch line is always when God says it's OK for Gypsies to steal from the rest of us, presumably because there are no more Roman soldiers to torment.

By the fifteenth century, the Gypsies were on the move, either under their own steam or as captives. While they called themselves *Lords of Egypt*, others soon referred to them instead as kidnappers, sexual offenders and even witches. It was during this time they were dubbed *Gypsies* (as in Egypt), and out of that came the word *gypped*. Being tortured for these real or imagined offenses caused the group to adopt an air of secrecy, often denying even their nationality. This us-against-them mentality exists until this day.

European Gypsies

This mostly illegal immigrant population arrived in the sixties, coming through Canada and Mexico with phony passports. They speak Rom, as well as several European languages and English—but only when it suits them. Bunco cops divide these former Iron Curtain natives into two basic groups, definable by ethnic origin as well as crime.

Yugoslavian Store-Diversion Suspects

Of the fifty-five Yugoslavian Gypsy families thought to be in the United States, fifty-four of them live within ten miles of Skokie, Illinois, and several within blocks of Skokie PD Detective Gary Nolte, considered to be one of the foremost authorities on this group today.

Within their culture, marriages are arranged at about age thirteen, and it's not unusual for a teenager to have as many as three small children. Considered second-class citizens, women best not talk while a man is flapping his lips, lest he stop and put her in her place before continuing. Because this closed society has only several hundred members, there's a lot of inbreeding, as evidenced by the inordinate amount of physical defects, crossed eyes, Down's syndrome and the like. Unlike the American Gypsies, most *Yugos* live off arterial streets, and their children attend at least some public schooling, sometimes even into the secondary grades.

Like all good gypsies, Yugos love to wander. When embarking on a crime spree, they either fly to a destination and rent a car, or travel in caravans displaying bent or obscured Illinois plates, keeping in touch via CB radios and cellular phones. Frequenting budget motels along the interstate, they target franchises like Builders Square, Home Depot, Kmart and minimarts where cookie-cutter blueprints insure a familiar setup in each location.

Eastern European Burglary Suspects

Made up of Polish, Russian and other illegal immigrants, this group is based mostly in New York City, Chicago and Ottawa. Again, they travel in teams (driving four-door vehicles with Illinois, New York, New Jersey or Virginia plates, or Alamo or Hertz rental cars that they trade in at frequent intervals) and stay at inexpensive motels along the interstate. They commit their crimes—often mailing the goods home in bubble packs—and travel to their next destination, often several hundred miles away, by nightfall.

The Crimes

Yugoslavian Gypsies specialize in store diversions, shoplifting, and dwelling burglaries in which they often trick the elderly in order to gain entry. While Gypsies are traditionally considered to be nonviolent, lately the Yugos have been displaying the "fight to flee" syndrome, turning a simple burglary into an armed robbery.

Eastern European burglary suspects specialize in dwelling burglaries and shoplifting only. Again the targets are upper-middle-class senior communities, and the most popular items taken are currency, jewelry, Oriental rugs and furs.

Store Diversions

Several out-of-control consumers distract employees by demanding service, asking nonsensical questions, complaining about goods or just being ornery. When wary personnel suspect a shoplifting in progress and respond accordingly, they fail to recognize the real con. It isn't the merchandise the Gypsies are after, it's the money in the day safe.

Knowing most safes are kept on "day set" where the combination takes only a twist to open, the perps take only some of the cash, thereby delaying discovery of the crime. These thefts are committed in broad daylight, with some groups grabbing the surveillance tape on their way out, and others snatching the entire camera. They leave as if on signal, one vehicle carrying the money, with only the driver visible. If capture seems imminent, often a Gypsy woman will toss her skirt up over her head, throwing the *gadji* (non-Gypsy) personnel into a tailspin and assuring the getaway.

Because nothing visible is gone, it is often several hours before the theft is discovered. When it is, the staff scurries around in a panic, contaminating the crime scene and often even fingering one of their own for the loss.

Are store diversions profitable? Out of just thirty-eight the National Association of Bunco Investigators (NABI) was able to track during a one-year period, the average hit was $15,000.

Shoplifting

Gypsies never do anything solo, and this activity is certainly no exception. As the traditional swarming diversionary tactic occurs, other shop(lift)ers expand in girth as jewelry, bolts of fabric, clothing and even bedding disappears up their skirts and into a "booster" apron. If they are caught, the apron is rarely recognized for what it is, a tool of the trade (important to establish intent), especially when wrapped around a head, as is done to hide it in plain sight. Since shoplifting is a low-priority offense, even if caught, these suspects can easily slip through the criminal justice system.

Dwelling Burglaries

These home invasions are frequently accomplished by the suspects conning their way inside a home rather than the traditional breaking and entering. Usually, a male will drive two or three females into a neighborhood and wait several streets away while the women work the 'hood. The suspects will take only the money and best jewelry, leaving everything else undisturbed, again delaying the discovery of the theft. Of the 210 dwelling burglaries NABI was able to determine exact losses for in 1996, the average was $41,753 per offense.

There are several possible scenarios:

- If an elderly person is in the yard, one woman will distract him while the others sneak inside.

- If an elderly person is inside (clues to owner's age are lace curtains, "My grandson is an honor student" bumper stickers, venetian blinds, etc.), one will knock, using a ruse to gain entry. Ploys include feigning illness, requesting a drink of water, asking to leave a note for a neighbor, inquiring if their child can use the bathroom, questioning if the house is for sale, or seeking help in looking for a lost pet. Once inside, the first woman will distract the homeowner while another, or a child, will commit the theft. (One of NABI's most colorful stories involves an elderly man waking up and finding a suspect going through his dresser drawers. When he asked what she was doing, she answered, "I am looking for my little dog.")

- If no one is home, the suspects will simply enter an unlocked door, break a window or jimmy a lock.

American Gypsies

These second- and third-generation Americans have been here longer that the European Gypsies and so are more modern, both in their dress and in the offenses they commit. The first big influx arrived in this country through Ellis Island, around the turn of the century. When the first groups were turned away for admitting they were Gypsies, subsequent immigrants began describing themselves as Greek, Portuguese, etc. Again, continuing another tradition.

Although many speak Rom, all but the very old speak English. In order to keep their children from assimilating into mainstream society, they attend no school at all, accounting for the 95 percent illiteracy rate. One Gypsy friend tells of living in various tent cities until the day his parents sued a property owner and ended up with a home of their own. Once the truant officer was able to make regular visits, he and his siblings began making friends and when he refused to steal from them, it was the beginning of the end for that particular *familya*. Now a contractor, he is quite the stellar feller.

The Identifiers

Gypsies change not only their names but their dates of birth (DOB) and Social Security numbers (SSN) with alarming frequency. One slick family we've investigated has their car registered in one name, their phone in another and their apartment in a third. Planning ahead, this couple even had the foresight to have their children delivered under aliases. An investigator's first Gypsy case is always a nightmare because these offenders don't follow the same "rules" *gadji* criminals do—like keeping a first name, DOB or at least initials, when creating an alias. Still, once you get the hang of it, it feels like you're chasing the same crook over and over. And often you are.

The Names

Gypsies have no loyalty to a name, and often several members of the group will use the same moniker to cause confusion. I personally know of six Sam Ways and four Pizza Yonkos. It doesn't help that the description of each is *dark and swarthy*.

- **The surname.** This can often be switched for the first, for example, Frank Tom and Tom Frank. Most Gypsy names are all-American and easily spellable like Adams, Frank and John. Now obviously, many *gadji* have these monikers, as well. But a cop's first question when determining if the suspect is Gypsy is, "What's the name?" If the answer is "Fred Adams," it could go either way. If "Pizza Yonko," then most would say, certainly.

- **The first name.** In defiance of the simplicity factor, many ladies can't resist such exotic epithets as Ruby, Silvia and Angela. There are also a lot of nicknames bantered about, Peaches, Giggles and, of course, Pizza, so called apparently because her complexion resembles a slice of pepperoni.

- **The middle name.** Until very recently, Gypsies never took one since the very reason middle names exist is to eliminate confusion.

The Date of Birth

Obviously they have one, they just rarely use it. When randomly choosing another, it's often something easy to remember, January 1 or July 4, for example. Others are picked out of the air with no concern about recall since inconsistency works in their favor. Most don't even bother to stay relatively the same age, making it all the more difficult to identify them.

The Social Security Number

Many are appropriated from dead victims. Not that Gypsies normally kill people, but since their victims are in their eighties and nineties, SSNs do become available on a regular basis. Unbelievably, this is one of the only areas where we've found Gypsies to trip up. By confiscating their victims' names and SSNs, they leave a road map of their past victims.

Common Denominators Among Gypsy Crime

Gypsy crime is easily identifiable because of the similar MOs. In fact, so universal are many factors that no thinking cop could fail to call this organized crime—on a grand, grand scale.

First of all, Gypsies are social. Insurance scams, fortune-telling swindles, store diversions, home repair frauds, even sweetheart swindles all require a team to pull off. Often they use their children as a front, either by giving them that look of legitimacy, or by actually involving the kids in the crime or diversion.

Since Gypsies are superstitious, flat-out believing in witches, demons, bad luck, the evil eye and the like, most of their crimes are committed in broad daylight rather than at night. How superstitious are the Rom? One Gypsy described her ex-husband as mute due to a curse she'd personally bestowed, and sure enough, when the cop caught up with him, the hubby couldn't talk, so convinced was he that he was no longer able to do so.

Until very recently, the American Gypsies rarely committed violent crimes. This is not to say the Rom don't shoot and stab one another, but their brutality toward outsiders has been limited to a few cases of suspected poisonings and placing a curse on my laptop computer. However, experts agree we're seeing more homicides, assaults and robberies as our civilization in general becomes more violent. Now when a victim attempts to detain the suspect, Gypsies are more likely to go into the "fight to flee" mode. In some cases, elderly victims have been tied up, knocked down, strangled and even had their oxygen masks lifted off their faces so they could better tell where they kept their valuables.

Gypsies play by their own rules. Since they marry in their own tribal ceremonies, they file no documents with Vital Statistics, making it difficult, for example, for a DA to prove bigamy when they marry a victim during the commission of a sweetheart scam (which they consider to be a simple business transaction).

Crimes Perpetrated by Females

In the Gypsy culture, it is the women who really bring home the bacon. While the men garner maybe $12,000 for a roofing scam, a sweetheart swindle can reap much more than that, up to a cool million and beyond. Yes, there is some crossover. Should you happen into a fortune-telling *officia* while the maid's away, it's not likely the hubby will turn you away, but you'll probably leave with the feeling you attended the opera the night the diva was out sick.

Fortune-Telling

Maria Valdadez went to see Mrs. Wellington about her unmanageable teenage daughter. During the initial visit, Maria was told to place a tomato in her bed and bring it back on her return visit. When she did, the psychic cut open the veggie and pulled out a skull. *Ugggghhhh.*

The tomato thing, though impressive, didn't prevent Maria's daughter from running away from home. Mrs. Wellington's solution to that was to burn up Maria's $16,000 nest egg—since money is, of course, the root of all evil. When that didn't help, she then told Maria to buy her a $40,000 trailer. I forget the reasoning.

Well, that made Maria a *little* suspicious. The cops confirmed Mrs. Wellington was actually Dorothy Demetro, three-time arrestee for the failure of removing similar curses. Her penance? Being charged with misdemeanor theft.

What's really happening? The $20 tarot or palm-reading fee is just chump change. The real income comes from eliminating all those horrid curses. The tomato (or egg) trick is accomplished via sleight of hand, a bit of hair and a Cracker Jack prize. In a dirty *officia*, clients routinely find themselves plagued with curses, the removal of which involves the burning of the $90 candles, having their life savings torched (switched) or even getting it buried in a nearby cemetery. The game continues as long as the client continues to play and pay.

The *officia* itself plays a paramount part in creating the illusion something mystical is about to occur. My chief investigator and I were once greeted by a two-hundred-pound seven-year-old we came to call Crystal Boy. With his sweatpants down below his crack, he never once uttered a word, instead choosing to toss a grapefruit-sized crystal ball around like a juggler and climbing over the furniture with the agility of an acrobat. Always intelligence gathering, Ann purred, "What's your name?" only to be given the evil eye, a sight so disconcerting we cut our reconnaissance short to fly back to the office and take sponge baths in the sink. It was shortly afterward that my laptop computer started malfunctioning.

This so-called psychic ability is actually a heightened sense of street smarts, which I believe compensates for their illiteracy, much the way the blind have intensified their other senses. Via "cold-reading" the patron's body language, they are able to dispense such inside knowledge as: "You're misunderstood." (Aren't we all?) "You're troubled." (Or you wouldn't be here.) "You've not been recognized for your genius." (Tell me.) Anybody can do it. Someone who's been doing it ten times a day for ten years can do it really well.

In every major city, you will see at least one open-palmed hand displayed on a major drag, beckoning newly arrived Rom to come learn who's the "Gypsy cop" and shyster of choice. Although this particular *officia* will stay relatively clean, most other parlors will come and go faster than disgruntled clients arrive with cops in tow.

Psychic Hot Lines

More and more Rom are abandoning the family *officias* for the safety of the profitable 800 or 900 numbers you see advertised in the tabloids.

Detective Sergeant Roy House (retired) of the Houston PD's Swindle Detail says he once did an informal study by calling all the numbers in the back of a supermarket tabloid. In every case but one, he found himself talking directly to a Rom.

Originally, says House, the Gypsies were simply employees hired for their convincing bubble-talk, but when they discovered how profitable (and safe) psychic hot lines were, the more sophisticated of their populace purchased the lines directly. And do the celebrities who endorse these lines know? I asked. House says they either don't know the ramifications or have simply sold their souls for the sake of a buck.

Again, we are talking curse-removal scams. The perp starts by asking name and date of birth, saying the caller should phone back after they've had a chance to do their chart. On the next $3.99-per-minute call, the person begins to unload themselves. Soon they actually do feel better, mostly because someone is finally giving some credence to their troubles.

Being experts in human nature, the Rom are able to assess just how much time is required to establish the person's trust, whether it be hours, days, weeks or even months. That accomplished, the psychic relates how things are far worse than previously predicted. In fact, there's a dreadful curse on the caller's life that can be zapped only by wiring their root-of-all-evil cash for the traditional cleansing. Sometimes the money is even returned—strictly to gain additional confidence—but there will always be requests for more. House says a victim losing $75,000 within the course of a year is not unusual.

Sweetheart Scams

Although sweetheart scams are committed by men and women of all nationalities, the Gypsy takes this business to a new art form. Who else watches from an upstairs window, running down to greet every old-timer who passes with the line that they are old friends, he just can't remember? In this heartbreaking scam, these seventy-, eighty- and ninety-somethings are often stalked until an "accidental" meeting can occur. After a honeymoon of companionship and take-out food, the old-timer is bilked and abandoned, leaving him too embarrassed to report the abuse, too blind to identify his honey, too befuddled to testify and too lovesick to even accept what's happened to him.

There are several consistent elements in a Gypsy sweetheart scam.

- The victims are (almost) always men, midseventies on up, and the perp a twenty- to fifty-year-old female.

- The victims are "tested" to determine their dementia. The most prolific pickup line is, "Don't you remember me? My mother used to bring me to visit you when I was a little girl." Victims buy into this so well that long after they've come to accept the con, they still believe they have known the person for years. As for how they're chosen, one inside source says Gypsies follow all old-timers to get a physical location and then have a naive or downright disreputable private eye run an asset check.

- The victims usually aren't what is considered wealthy, but they always have assets of some sort, a nest egg, property, even credit. All old men are chosen, the game just goes on longer for men with more.

- Even sweetheart scams are a team effort, the profits split among the *familya*. Traditionally, there's an advance person who determines the target, a "brother" who is actually the husband, and an entire extended family that rounds out the false reality.

- There is an initial test request, almost always a car. Subsequent pleas involve health crises and start-up businesses. Since Gypsies are loathe to pay for anything themselves, victims often end up subsidizing the whole family's phones, groceries and even the pager that keeps him at beeper length.

- At some point, "sex" is introduced, consisting mostly of a little bosom flashing and fondling. For a man widowed thirty years, this alone is a heart attack in the making. But the sex, as we dicussed in chapter three, serves a more basic purpose. Faced with what their nineteenth-century ethics renders an illicit relationship, these men keep their "dirty little secret," often right up to the point when they marry. And how can a gentleman of this rearing *not* marry when he has participated in such hanky-panky?

- Marrying a victim is the Gypsy equivalent of winning the lottery, yet unlikely to occur unless there's a property involved. The real estate quickly transfers to a joint tenancy deed, allowing it to pass to the Gypsy bride upon the victim's death without having to go through probate.

- The new wife never comes to live with her husband, citing temporary family problems or whatever. In all, she will never spend more than a few sporadic nights at his home.

- The scam continues for years and isn't over until the elder is bled dry or some heroic party steps in to obtain a conservatorship over him. Even then, the Gypsy bride hovers about, insuring her honey won't cooperate with the authorities.

How prolific is this abomination? At the time of this writing, we personally know of over thirty ongoing cases in the Bay area. In all, the old man either has lost everything or is in the process of doing so—and we just can't seem to stop it. Our first such case was profiled on a 1993 segment of *20/20*, in the December 1, 1997, issue of *Newsweek*, and in the true-crime book *Hastened to the Grave*, by Edgar Award-winning author Jack Olsen. In this particular instance, the first cousins of our perps were simultaneously pulling the same scam in

New York City, right down to using the same drug to expedite their victim's demise.

Crimes Perpetrated by Males

And now for the boys. As you might expect, their scams are a bit more manly.

Auto Repair

Our office neighbor fell for an auto bonding scheme. The bonding was completed in less than fifteen minutes, and afterward her car looked like a tin can smothered in giant silver Band-Aids. Yet she never once thought to call the cops, since they'd provided a service. And so however slipshod, she felt she had no recourse. By the time the bonding fell off during the first rain, the Gypsies were long gone and their pager number disconnected.

About that same time, our favorite plumber allowed his nice new truck to be spread with bonding gunk, the Gypsies using a piece of cardboard as a spreading tool. When it came time to pay, the $400 estimate had doubled, presumably because he'd insisted on quality. For him we dialed 911, but clearly the San Francisco PD did not consider illegal car repair a priority. An officer arrived thirty-five minutes later, a long time when you're trying to outtalk a Gypsy. The cop never got out of his car, just called out from across the street, inquiring if everything was all right. Clearly intimidated, the plumber could not confidently voice his concerns, and so the cop took down the plate number *of the victim* and drove off.

OK, shoddy bodywork happens daily in every American city, so what makes Gypsy auto bonding any different? A reputable shop uses the time-consuming process of spreading layers on thinly, allowing them to dry between applications. Since a Gypsy cannot claim a parking space that long, he globs the gunk on in one fell swoop. Not only can it not be smoothed out properly, it's only a matter of time before the still-wet compound falls out in chunks.

How do Gypsies target their victims? Most just cruise the streets, yelling out their windows at drivers. Now what consumer wouldn't think they were getting a deal with overhead so low they have no shop?

Home Repair

A woman wrote to the "Ask Rat Dog" column, stating she'd discovered a check written by her seventy-three-year-old father to "Tom's Roofing" for $21,000. The outlet manager who cashed the draft described Fred Tom as a regular customer and a reputable businessman, adding he'd personally verified her dad's signature. Strange indeed, since her father lived four hundred miles away.

Typical home repair scam: Claiming to have leftover materials from a nearby job, this Gypsy quoted a price based solely on his off-the-cuff appraisal of the homeowner's worth and gullibility. Some work was done, although entirely cosmetic, and afterward the handyman declared the job was more involved than anticipated and therefore would cost more. Then, he cashed her dad's check at a check-cashing outlet and moved on.

What home repairs are we talking about? Driveway sealant that's either watered down or consists solely of automotive oil. Roofing repairs that consist of slathering on the very same oil. Foundation repairs, tree trimming and pruning, electrical and plumbing work, septic tank pumping, and pest extermination. All of inferior quality.

Unfortunately, this was not the last we'd see of Fred Tom. His family resurfaced during our investigation of a sweetheart scam, and at the time of this writing, neither crime has been prosecuted.

Utility Inspector Con

Here the perp poses as a meter reader in order to gain entry into the house. That done, he enlists the homeowner's help, thereby diverting him while his cohorts commit burglary. (More on this in the section on Travelers below.)

Vehicle Sales Con

After a staged accident, the Gypsy gets rid of the car, either by rolling back the odometer to increase its value, or simply selling it twice over and then disappearing.

Metal Thefts

A business owner is asked to donate scrap metal for a charitable cause. While the metal is being removed from the business, other undonated items are disappearing, as well.

Caretaker Con

In this genderless, romanceless sweetheart scam, all the other money-grabbing elements are present. In one case, a male Gypsy struck up a friendship with an eighty-five-year-old alcoholic by commenting they had the same last name. After he moved in, my chief investigator and I got wind of it and persuaded a private conservator to petition the court for conservatorship. On a subsequent visit, we found the older gent had "misplaced" his passport and checkbook. While the conservator made chitchat, Ann and I took a stroll down to the Gypsy's room and there found the missing items.

Was he ever arrested and/or prosecuted? No can do, said the PD. Since we stopped the crime before it was committed, there was no loss and therefore no victim. The fact that the Gypsy had forged three checks on the old man's account didn't change their opinion.

Crimes Perpetrated by Both Sexes

Although the specifics may differ by gender, the basic scams remain the same.

Home Invasions

In 1995, the Huntington, California PD finally nabbed a trio of faux utility workers who'd terrorized their community for over three years. It was the Demetros again, this time Billy, 47; son Joseph, 20; and stepson Perry Tan, 19. Cops say they'd drive around all day until they saw an elderly person through a window or on a porch, then stop and point out a needed repair. If the victim declined, the men would return later, posing as utility workers. As one checked out the power, gas or whatever, the others helped themselves to the goodies inside.

Poor memories and/or eyesight hindered the investigation for a while, but once someone was able to provide a description of the suspects' car, cops were able to tail it, collecting six hours' worth of witnesses/victims along the way and making an arrest. The resulting sting netted more than seven hundred rare coins, five hundred pieces of jewelry, a wall safe and a bunch of pawnshop tickets. One single victim had lost $62,000 in cash and valuables.

But home invasions are not always a nonviolent crime. In one extreme case, an elderly woman was tied up with phone cords and left in her unheated house for three days before being discovered by neighbors. Had she died, it would have undoubtedly been labeled a robbery gone wrong; however, she lived long enough to tell police it was a home invasion gone wrong.

Entry is routinely gained via a mother asking if her child can come in to use the bathroom (the child ransacks while mom chats), or even the roofer who's taking a break from his more labor-intensive swindle outside. In any case, in this team effort, one suspect chats while another pilfers.

Insurance Fraud: Slip and Falls

The most common Gypsy insurance scams are staged accidents, lost luggage, slip and falls, and renter's insurance. For more on insurance fraud, see chapter sixteen.

In one case, during an investigation of a Gypsy woman who was quite successfully bilking an eighty-seven-year-old man out of $475,000, we found, via a practice application in her trash, that her son was applying for a minimum-wage job at a fast-food joint. Just a tad skeptical that this illiterate boy had chosen a life of minimum wage, we called the gas station he'd listed as a reference and found the phone answered with a distinct Romany accent. Checking the Plaintiff/Defendant's index, we discovered a lawsuit for a slip and-fall accident involving the fast-food chain, wherein our suspect's son was listed as an employee who'd witnessed the accident. Coinky-dink? I don't think so. Insurance experts confirmed this particular chain was known to settle all claims ASAP, spending as little as possible on litigation and, of course, investigation.

Insurance Fraud: Staged Accidents

Eighty-five-year-old Mabel Terse was going fifteen miles per hour when a car started honking at her from behind. Mabel grew increasingly nervous as the folks inside yelled for her to stop and then accused her of hitting them, backing up their claim with a long black mark alongside both cars. The occupants came swarming about, insisting she was too old to drive and threatening to call the police. On the spot, she wrote them a check for the $1,000 deductible and took their suggestion not to report the incident to her insurance company.

What really happened? The "scratch" came from a black felt-tipped marker, and Mabel's name was passed along to other family members for further swindles.

Beating the Heat

Since they have long been committing—and occasionally even getting caught for—the proceeding abuses, these ultimate survivors have learned how to best deal with the criminal justice system. Going to any extreme to avoid incarceration, Gypsies will claim not to speak English and will give out bogus names and identifiers.

In the past, Gypsies have misrepresented themselves as police officers, judges, doctors and even attorneys in order to get inside information, arrange bail reduction hearings and even attempt to convince the court that the suspect cannot stand trial due to a medical condition.

Traditionally, one local well-connected attorney will handle all Gypsy squabbles, using his vast political powers and influence on behalf of his clients. A bail bondsman is also a closely maintained associate.

Gypsies consider the paying back of some monies to be the price of doing business, and cash is set aside for this purpose. Sometimes the restitution is offered in court—a suitcaseful, one-time settlement. Other times, it's presented through a private investigator, attorney or local Gypsy. Without admitting guilt, the representative suggests that although the suspect is innocent, everyone in the Gypsy community is so upset about the victim's loss that they all pitched in to help him out. Unless the restitution is made through the court, more often than not the victim will find himself talked down on the amount and then even shortchanged on that.

Other tactics are for the suspect to act as an informant in exchange for charges being dropped, or plead for someone from law enforcement to intercede by citing past informant helpfulness, or simply offer a bribe. Suspects will promise to vacate the jurisdiction and never return, the clan will insure the deportation, and the not-so-idle threat will be made that if the suspects are forced to remain in the area pending trial, they will commit even more crimes in the meantime.

If the prosecution proceeds, Gypsies try to get cases postponed as long as possible, knowing many of the elderly victims will not live long enough to attend trial.

Travelers

These thirty-thousand fair-haired and fair-skinned Irish, English and Scottish Travelers (or "Tinkers") melt more easily into the mainstream than the Rom and so are often not even recognized as being a part of a secretive and elusive clan. Travelers have more education than the Rom; boys attend school through the eighth grade, and girls usually quit after the sixth, at which time the youngsters join together in dowry-driven unions.

The Scottish Travelers

Settling in Cincinnati in the early 1800s, this largest group of Travelers is known for home repair cons and sales fraud. They are often called the Terrible Williamsons, for their most active family.

The English Travelers

There is no single home base for this clan when they are not traveling the United States peddling inferior services such as driveway paving, home repair cons, painting, impostor and sales frauds.

The Irish Travelers

Probably the best known because of the three thousand based in South Carolina's unincorporated Murphy Village, their cons of choice are house and barn painting, tool sales frauds, roof coating and lightning rod sales.

Murphy Village is comprised of some three hundred huge and gaudy houses, three groceries and a couple of gambling trailers. Sharing only eleven major surnames, the Travelers use outsiders' ignorance of nicknames like Cracker Jack to confound reporters, police and bill collectors.

Irish Traveler history dates back to the potato famine when massive evictions developed a subculture of itinerant tinkers forced to traverse Ireland, sleeping in wagons or tents. In the late 1840s, Tom Carrol immigrated to New York, and within fifty years his descendants were trading horses and mules throughout the Southeast. After a 1927 Georgia law required them to pay $250 in taxes in every county where they did business, they started selling inferior floor coverings instead. By the 1950s, they'd added tractor sales and barn painting to their repertoire, and about 1980, they began peddling shop equipment.

Their Crimes

In all three clans, the men work the northern states during the summer and the sunbelt states in the winter, targeting "country people," as they refer to the rest of us, with their substandard home repair scams, utility inspector gags and tool sales fraud. These ill-gotten gains are often invested in legitimate enterprises such as trailer parks, trailer distributorships and even church ownerships. Bunco cops speculate these legitimate enterprises allow them tax shelters, meeting places, and even a way to facilitate laundering money.

When spotting these groups, cops typically watch for their new or well-cared-for pickup trucks topped with caps with side-locking windows, spraying equipment, religious paraphernalia and removable magnetic signs.

Home Repair Fraud

Travelers target elderly homeowners, offering a low-cost tree pruning service. When the bill is presented, the elderly person discovers the quote was per limb, not per tree.

Another ploy is to tell the homeowner they have left-over materials from another roofing, painting or driveway sealant job nearby and so can offer a bargain price. They use bogus or diluted materials, cut with gasoline or kerosene, and the job is finished in a matter of minutes. All this done, they insist on a higher payment. Using similar sales tactics, the Traveler offers to spray away offending pests, real or invented. Here's how Traveler Jimmy Burke describes roofing à la Traveler in Don Wright's 1996 book *Scam! Inside America's Con Artist Clans.*

> Now the stuff that the Travelers put on roofs don't do nothin' except just color it. We'll go to the store and buy a five-gallon bucket of the cheapest kind of driveway sealer we can find. We'll dump it in a tank and then pour in twenty-five gallons of water with it and add the contents of a fifty-five-gallon drum of aluminum paste. The paste ain't nothin' but a color. It's really thick, but when we mix it with the sealer, all it does is turn that stuff silver. The mixture is as thin as water, but when it's put on a roof, it dries instantly and looks great. All it does, though, is color the roof. The people get the impression that it's goin' to stop all their leaks, but it don't. It won't seal nothin'.

Sales Fraud

Offering a free inspection, Travelers will find that lightning rods are faulty and need to be "repaired" or replaced. Travelers known as *Jackers* will sell inferior tools with bogus warranties.

Trailer Sales

My first introduction to the Traveler community came from the viewpoint of a near-victim. At the time, a friend and I were in the market for a secondhand trailer, something to park on a small piece of property we jointly owned. One day while driving there, we passed what looked like a brand-new trailer with a for-sale sign. I called and got voice mail, and my call was returned from another nearby area code. When I called that number, it went to a Holiday Inn. Right away, I smelled a con.

My friend and I were met by a woman, her husband, their teenage son and a grandma, all speaking with a quirky Scottish accent. The trailer still had the plastic over the furniture and was probably $5,000 undervalued. Their story was they'd come from Oklahoma because their friends had done so well out here in the West. Originally, they were going to live in the trailer, but since the contractor/husband had been presented with a partnership opportunity, they decided to sell it for some quick cash. In fact, we were asked to write the check directly to the new partner, because there wasn't time for it to clear Pop's account.

When questioned about his unusual lilt, Dad claimed he was American born and bred, of Scottish descent. By now I was fairly certain these were Travelers, but I had yet to study the group in any detail. It must have been an awfully tight family, I silently mused, for Dad to have retained the accent of his ancestors rather than his schoolmates and community. Another curiosity was that the family was paying perhaps $70 per night for a hotel room, rather than $250 per month in a trailer park.

Even though the pink slip looked authentic, I began researching the manufacturer, first in a nationwide phone disc, then in 800 number directory assistance, and finally at the public library in a reference book on trailer manufacturing. Not surprisingly, the brand didn't seem to exist. Later, at a NABI conference, I learned more about this exclusively Traveler scam, thought to exceed $30 million annually.

No, the trailers aren't stolen. They are constructed in Elkhart, Indiana, by legitimate manufacturers who ignore all federal requirements regarding plumbing, appliances and electrical systems. These aesthetically pleasing tin cans have been sold "out the back door" to Travelers ever since the Arab oil embargo threatened the economy in the eighties. To establish the original price, the buyer gets a "factory invoice," which is actually just an option list touting the highest possible suggested retail price. It's not unusual for a $3,200 trailer to have a factory invoice suggesting it was originally purchased for $12,000.

In Wright's *Scam!* he tells of two teenagers who broke into a trailer manufacturing plant and made off with a safe containing $60,000. They then took a road trip, paying for gas and food with $100 bills and, when change couldn't be made, leaving the rest behind with confused and concerned clerks all the way to Florida. Following this trail—many reported it because they feared the money was counterfeit—the authorities finally caught up with them and obtained a confession.

When the police sergeant went to return the $44,000 they confiscated, he was shocked to learn the plant owner had not reported the theft. When directly questioned, the owner claimed the safe was empty when it was stolen. It was the prosecutor who figured out that these manufacturers would rather lose the cash than explain how they got it by ignoring federal manufacturing guidelines, and how they kept it by not reporting it to the IRS. The punch line is that the kids got to keep the money, because nobody could ever prove they got it illegally.

Utility Inspector Con

A person representing himself as a water, gas or electrical company employee either diverts the homeowner's attention so his accomplices can pilfer whatever currency and/or jewelry can be found, or sells him a substandard service or product he doesn't need. Neighborhoods of elderly residents are most often hit, frequently the same folks who have earlier been targeted by home improvement scammers. The utility inspector con is a specialty of both Gypsies and Travelers, and the perps will work a region until they have either milked it dry or been curtailed by a wave of nasty publicity.

Of the twenty-four utility impostor crimes NABI was able to determine exact losses for in 1996, it found the average hit to be $35,565. Of course, most of these crimes are never reported, and many are never even identified as utility inspector gags by cops not versed in Gypsy and Traveler crime.

The perps traditionally gain access to a premises by

- Claiming the homeowner is due a refund of some sort. While the mark is making change for the "inspector's" $100 bill, the elder is actually showing the crooks where he keeps his money.

- Claiming a faulty water meter must be replaced, and even threatening to cut off the water if a new unit is not purchased.

- Inspecting for water damage and then secretly spraying a wall to convince the homeowner there's a leak.

- Instructing the homeowner to go to the basement to turn

on a faucet or to the backyard to see an area that needs repair. While the homeowner is thus diverted, the other suspects are robbing the house.

- Claiming they need to inspect the property's lot line. This requires the citizen's help, specifically to hold one end of a string while they take the other end around the corner and out to the street. What's really happening? They tie it to a tree and help themselves to the nice stuff inside.

Insurance Fraud

One of the best depictions of Traveler life ever was a *Dateline* piece produced by Sandra Surles and reported by Lea Thompson in which three young Irish Travelers staged a rape at a Disney World hotel.

It was Halloween 1992, and a man in a Dracula costume had been seen hanging around the Caribbean Beach Resort. Later, that same man was thought to have gained entry into twenty-year-old Wanda Mary Burke Normile's room, tied her up with duct tape, beat her with a wooden club and raped her. The cops bought her story, and why wouldn't they since the crime scene was consistent with her tale? The ninety-eight-pound victim was covered with bruises, and tests confirmed there had been sexual intercourse.

They were still haggling over a settlement when Wanda Mary's sister Jessee confessed that brother Jimmy had thought the whole scheme up after watching a television report on Disney's lack of hotel security. Dressed conspicuously as Dracula, Jimmy had approached maids with the story that he'd left his hotel key in the room. Nobody fell for it, but it did get Jimmy remembered, thus upping the hotel's liability. Wanda Mary did her part, as well, allowing herself to get beaten to a pulp and having intercourse with her uncle's friend prior to the incident. Jessee was merely the sister who made Wanda Mary's stay in the hotel plausible.

On *Dateline*, Wanda Mary called it "the perfect con." Disney was ready to settle, to the tune of $3 million, when Jessee became unhappy with the proposed split and ratted out her sibs. Now on parole, Wanda Mary was asked on-air what was going through her mind when her brother was "beating the tar" out of her. Replied the Traveler, "Everybody was going to talk about it for generations. It was going to be . . . I was going to be a legend."

Instead, Wanda Mary came out of jail with a twenty-year parole that not only restricts her to the county in which she resides, but forbids her from frequenting Disney World, as it was not located in that county. Jimmy died of AIDS before he could be apprehended.

POWERFUL PREDATORS

"It's always better to have something happen to you than nothing happen to you."

—Something I no longer say

This chapter is all about those perps who use their position of power to toy with the victims' emotions in order to obtain their assets. They are the men and women who use their sexual prowess to manipulate another's assets, who prey on the misfortune of others by falsely claiming they have the power either to heal physical or emotional wounds, or to find missing persons. They are the sweetheart scammers, the phony psychics, the faith healers and those who just flat-out grift the grieving.

Sweetheart Scams

Sometimes it's for sex, sometimes for money, but what makes a sweetheart scam different from just plain dating is heavy petting under false pretenses. The perps can be perpetual big-amists, inmates trolling for intimates, or lethal-minded lovers. The pigeons might be met by chance, stalked, or even solicited through the classifieds or the Internet. Whatever the circumstance, the result is always victims stripped of their dignity, naïveté, belief in their fellow human beings and, of course, their assets.

This is not to say sweetheart scammers are without a certain charm. And since their glib persuasive nature is their primary tool of the trade, the lesser the development of their conscience, the more charming they'll appear.

The pigeons also fit a profile. Whether they're professional businesspersons who "ought to know better" or single moms on public assistance, every one of them is vulnerable to attention and wants to believe in love. They also each have something to offer, even if it's just enough credit to get a phone in their own name.

May-December Romances

Anna Nicole Smith did it and everybody laughed. Marrying a man old enough to play chess with her grandpa made her night-show fodder, but the nationwide story hits too close to home to be humorous to this detective agency. Although wealthy men often marry younger women as "trophy wives," where this activity crosses the line is when the gent's old enough to forget what the word *dementia* means. That is called financial elder abuse, and for the perfect example see "Mr. K. Takes a Bride" in the chapter entitled "The Ten-Step Program to Plotting a Con."

The Murphy Man

This con was named after the many Irish guys who fell for it. Paddy was a young merchant marine on leave in San Francisco, his pockets full and looking for love in a neighborhood internationally known for such outings. Along comes a "pimp" who assures Paddy he can provide the girl of his dreams. Just name the race, age and bust size. Money changes hands but then a cop happens by, causing both bad boys to run for cover. After the trouble passes, Paddy reemerges, anxious for the fulfillment of the transaction, but the pimp fails to show.

What's really happening? Just a simple case of Paddy

getting no services rendered. The cop is either in on it, or his part is played by a plain-clothed impostor. Perpetrated on servicemen and visiting businessmen, this con is played in hotel lounges and touristy areas. For obvious reasons, it's rarely reported to the authorities.

The Badger Game

In a particularly funny episode of NBC's *Seinfeld*, George Costanza meets a woman on the subway who finally falls for his architect line, hook, line and sinker. He can't believe his good luck when she, with very little verbal fore-play, suggests they go to a hotel room together.

While George is phoning Jerry to convey his good luck, the beauty is in the bathroom "changing." What she's changing, of course, is the contents of George's wallet into her own. Out she comes fully dressed, taking both the wallet and George's clothes with her. Typical badger game, except that the norm involves a two-person team, with the man acting as "pimp."

Entrapment

Like George and Paddy, Marty was in the mood. Leav-ing his wife to ponder which client had kept him working late this particular evening, he frequented his favorite bar, picked up a willing partner and accompanied her back to her place. Just when things got interesting, who should show up but the "husband" whom she had neglected to mention.

Big altercation. During which Hubby grabs Marty's wallet, pockets his driver's license and declares he's going to call the other man's wife. Carefully, the cheating hubby is manipulated into suggesting that the very contents of that wallet might sooth the situation to the point where he can make a clean getaway.

Unfortunately, that's not the end of it. Soon Marty re-ceives pictures of the unfortunate compromise. Now realizing he's been set up from the very beginning, Marty's choices are to continue paying or risk exposure.

Variations on a theme:

- The "lady" runs a classified, looking for an unencum-bered sexual relationship. Those suitors who pen back their romantic musings have unwittingly provided the blackmailer with the evidence necessary to carry through the threat of exposure.

- The victim is lured into a compromising position with an "underage" girl. Suddenly comes the vice squad, willing to overlook the charge of statutory rape—for a price. What's really happening? Sometimes a crooked cop is in on it; more often, the plainclothesman has no uniform at all.

- The victim has neglected to tell his wife he prefers men, a fact that the perp now has evidence of.

- After sex, the lady thoroughly dishevels herself and screams rape.

A Dating Mistake

Barbara met Jeffrey in Boston's Back Bay when he stopped to ask directions, him being new in town and all. After having the local laundry, ATM, video store, etc. pointed out, her new neighbor asked her out on a date.

On that first rendezvous, Jeffrey had one small problem. The ATM had gobbled up his card, and it being the weekend, the banks were all closed. Barbara sprang for dinner with the assurance he'd gladly repay her Tuesday for the hamburgers they ate today.

Barbara quickly became Jeffrey's new best friend. The pal he called when his car got itself stolen. The shoulder he cried on when divorce/credit problems made his life suck. The bail bond gal he turned to when a cop mistakenly yanked his driver's license and threw his sorry butt in jail. The second time Jeffrey had his recurring ATM card-eating nightmare, he asked Barbara to access her own account for cash, which he dutifully reimbursed with a personal check. When his new employer neglected to issue him a company credit card, Barbara agreed to show hers to the hotel—for identification purposes only, mind you.

Soon Jeffrey was late for, sleepwalked through, or just simply didn't show up for most of their dates. There were always reasons, though, and very good ones. Like when he was incarcerated for driving without the license that mean cop yanked. Meanwhile, Barbara prepared home-cooked meals, bought him a Dad's Day gift (which he returned for cash) and continued to make herself physically available to him.

When Jeffrey's first check came back marked "no such account," he apologetically replaced it with another from a second account. When that came back likewise declined, Jeffrey took offense to her crankiness and hung up on her. Not only did Babs call back to apologize, she sent him a little "I'm Sorry" note, as well.

Soon the couple couldn't exchange word one without Barbara bringing up the money thing. Jeffrey's response was that maybe they shouldn't see each other anymore. Barbara sent him another carefully chosen card, but the damage was done. After that, Jeffrey simply didn't call anymore, and when she phoned, he was never there. Barbara had some residual feelings, of course. Hurt. Betrayal. Embarrassment. And, oh yes, that bit about the credit card.

Jeffrey's hotel confirmed he was still checked in. And yes, his lodging and expenses were indeed being charged to her credit card. Whoa! But how was that possible since the card was to be used for identification purposes only, and was at its limit when he'd checked in weeks ago? She cancelled the card and sent a certified letter to the hotel stating she'd done so. She called to confirm, and they acknowledged their receipt of her letter.

Regardless, three weeks later, the credit card company phoned to inform her she was $2,500 over her limit. Even more irksome, Jeffrey was still there, swilling bottles of Seagram's 7 Crown in his room with a view. The hotel claimed to have called for verification at each $300 increment and received authorization. They'd apparently done this four times *after* the card was cancelled. The credit card company insisted Barbara was liable, and only after a rather nasty note from her attorney did they back down.

Internet Entanglements

Sixteen-year-old Nicole had been corresponding for some time with Gus, whom she met via the Internet. Now

Nicole wanted to visit her aunt who lived near her twenty-five-year-old "millionaire" beau's hometown so she could finally meet the man of her mouse. Then there was Emily whose fellah was "an Emmy Award-winning rock musician" she met through America Online. And finally there was Karen, who tipped the scales at 240 in real life but was a "Heather Locklear look-alike" when obscured by her modem. These are just a few of the high-tech honeys we've investigated since E-mail romances have come full tilt. And unbelievably, out of all these, *not one* electronic suitor has lived up to his or her claims.

So yeah, these folks are liars, but are they con artists? In these cases, no money changed hands and no lives were lost, so I'd have to say no. Yet it does on occasion happen. And it does so primarily because of the inherently anonymous ambience of the medium. This unprecedented protector of privacy is sure to become the playground of con artists in all arenas, love included.

Prison Pen Pals

I pride myself on probably getting more letters from prison than any other noncelebrity in America. And why? Simply because my "Ask Rat Dog" column runs in newspapers that are delivered there daily. But while I may be easy fodder, the truth is men in prison cultivate any friendship they can with women on the outside. It seems to be the number one hobby in the Big House.

I might have gone on forever thinking the scam was that my suitors were simply not as nice and sweet and respectful and innocent as they claimed, had the U.S. Postal Inspector not set me straight. According to an Internet bulletin, my prisoner pals might actually be more interested in levying my bank account than in receiving my chatty letters.

Apparently, after gaining a woman's trust via a slew of love letters and bodybuilding photos, the prisoners will invariably ask for help with their personal troubles. A common request is that the lady deposit his $1,000 money order in her account, and then write the same amount to his attorney from her personal account.

What's really happening? The draft he gives her is actually a $1 cashier's check smuggled in by an accomplice and altered to read $1,000. After the draft goes back to be compared with the original, the discrepancy is discovered and her account is debited $1,000. The attorney, of course, is not listed with the bar association, and then comes the Dear Jane letter where the con says he's out of jail (he isn't) and no longer interested.

Phony Psychics

Psychic healers, spiritualists, fortune-tellers, psychic hot lines. Now, everyone has their own opinion as to whether there's anything to paranormal activity, but there's no arguing many "psychics" simply aren't, and are using their client's belief in the supernatural simply to line their own pockets.

Now, in all truthfulness, I would have to stop short of saying I flat-out don't believe in the paranormal. Who among us has not had the experience of thinking of someone and having the phone ring just then, with them on the line? Our own family history boasts the tale of great-great-grandmama "watching" her twin brother walk across the field when he should have been out fighting the Civil War, only to later learn he'd been killed at that exact moment.

But can ESP be summoned on demand when a customer arrives, cash in hand? Can hundreds of these specially gifted individuals be gathered together to staff a hot line when the calls are coming in faster than flapcakes are flipped at a fireman's breakfast? If psychic detectives really solve crimes, why doesn't even one U.S. police force have even one of these individuals on staff? Quite obviously, anyone can claim to foretell the future. And who's to prove them wrong? Usually, by the time the future rolls around, some facsimile of those generalities will have come to pass, possibly via the client's own self-fulfilling prophecy.

The Lingo

Psychic: One who professes paranormal powers like being able to mentally move objects, predict the future and read minds.

Spiritualist: One who claims to communicate with the dead by conjuring up the spirit's presence.

Medium: One who uses her body to house the spirit, often during a *seance* where the spirits demonstrate their presence by moving objects around or even showing up.

Channeler: A New Age term for a medium who houses from just one embodiment to a whole host of characters.

Fortune-teller: One who gives advice based on one of several specialties. An *astrologer* gives advice based upon the position of the stars and planets; a *cartomacist* upon how a deck of playing cards is dealt; a *numerologist* uses significant numbers in a person's life for their readings; a *tarot card reader, tea leaf reader, palm reader* and *crystal gazer* all give advice and predict the future based on those particular props.

The History

Modern spiritualism dates back to 1848 when two up-state New York sisters caused a sensation with their abilities to conjure up their household ghosts. People would come from miles around to behold the psychic powers of Katherine Fox, 11, and her sister Margaret, 13, and well into adulthood they reveled in that limelight. At some point, the Fox family moved from the old homestead, and so loyal were their goblins, they came with them. Well, they must have, because subsequent occupants noticed nothing that ever went bump in the night.

Then, as adults, for reasons of their own, the sibs elected to let the world in on their secret. First Kate was quoted as saying, "Spiritualism is a humbug from beginning to end. It is the greatest humbug of this century." Two weeks later, Margaret confirmed it had all been a ruse. She announced before a fascinated crowd at the New York Academy of Music that their infamous spirited clamorings were not communications from the beyond at all, but simply the thud of a swinging apple as it knocked against the floor, or the snapping of their toes against their wooden bed. Unfortunately, by then others had discovered the lucrative world of spiritualism and weren't about to back down just because their founders had come clean.

Whether there is anything of substance to spiritualism can be debated indefinitely. This section is not meant to disrespect those who are fanatic believers, only to put forth the way "psychics" scam believers.

Cold Readings

The technique behind all psychic shenanigans is the concept of *cold reading*, whereby the fortune-teller deciphers the client's body language, answers and mood to determine just what is bothering them and what they want to know.

First, it must be noted that people go to a psychic because they have a problem, usually falling under the general categories of things that disturb most people: love, money, career or family. After guessing which of the four they have come about, phony psychics often dispense such invaluable utterings as, "You should go with your heart," and "Nobody appreciates what you go through." Considered the art behind the scam, this reaction watching has gotten many a fortune-teller touted as "gifted."

In their highly quotable book *Sting Shift*, Lindsay E. Smith and Detective Bruce A. Walstad interviewed a Chicago banker who took up tarot card reading as a lark. Thomas Dobrowolski studied "for maybe a night," and then donned dark clothing, sunglasses and slicked-back hair to look the part. For props, he aged some tarot cards by smearing them with black shoe polish and scribbled some crib notes onto his wrist. Then he opened his door for business.

After his first readings, Dobrowolski realized he could pick up on things that were basically true, just from his clients' reactions. "They'd ask leading questions without even realizing it," he told the authors. Being basically a decent man, Dobrowolski stopped short of giving advice that would direct his clients' actions. If a woman asked should she divorce her husband, for example, he'd defer, saying she would have to make that decision herself.

Still, it wasn't long before Dobrowolski chose to end his fortune-telling career altogether. "The reason I got out was that I felt dirty," he said. "I saw ways to make a lot of money, but I didn't feel good about it. If you go in as a performer,

like a magician, and you do a show, everyone knows it's entertainment. They have a good time and they pay you. The problem with tarot card reading is that a lot of people don't view
this as entertainment, and I felt I was taking money under false
pretenses."

So was Dobrowolski alone in realizing his psychic powers were a put-on, or do all psychics consider themselves to
be con artists? The now-again banker puts the statistics at
about fifty-fifty. Half, says he, have deluded themselves into
thinking they actually have some kind of paranormal ability,
and the other half are just knowingly making this stuff up.

Psychic Surgery

Mrs. Remmington had cancer that cut her life expec-
tancy to a scant four months. The doctors offered little hope,
but a friend suggested she meet with a famous Filipino doctor
who was traveling across America demonstrating his psychic
healing ability, even as they spoke. Since Mrs. Remmington
had long been critical of the FDA for taking forever to ap-
prove European products and for discounting Eastern meth-
odologies in favor of more expensive procedures endorsed
by the American Medical Association (AMA), it didn't take
much to persuade her to give this doctor a try.

Unfortunately, by the time she located him, the doc had
already returned home. Undeterred, Mrs. R. was determined
to travel to the Philippines and become his patient. In a fax,
the doc promised his "surgery" would not result in any cutting, pain, scars or wounds. Instead, he would merely reach his
bare hands into her stomach and remove the diseased tumor.

For this once-energetic world traveler, psychic surgery
seemed a viable option. She had long been tolerant of other
cultures' time-honored methods of healing. If nothing else,
she bragged to friends, it would be "a last hurrah." One more
great adventure.

After a grueling travel schedule that further zapped her
energy, Mrs. Remmington arrived at the doctor's place of
business. It was not a clean and orderly clinic, as she'd expected, but a back room in his unpretentious house. Mrs.
R. was shown into the examining room and prepped by the

doctor's wife—a procedure that consisted of having holy water sprinkled onto her abdomen and rubbed around in a soothing motion. Eventually the doctor arrived, and after a few words of comfort, he began kneading the area. As he did so, Mrs. R. was surprised (and heartened) to see blood appear, spilling all over her abdomen. After five minutes of this, she felt pressure and was amazed to see the doctor's hand disappear into her stomach. Then up came his hand, pulling the malignancy with it in a showy, graphic, disgusting Kodak moment. After the cleanup of the stringy, bloody mess, she was amazed to see he'd kept his promise, there'd been no cuts or abrasions. The doctor triumphantly declared the operation a success and his patient healed.

Unfortunately, Mrs. Remmington felt no better. In fact, she was so weak, she put off her trip home for several days in order to recuperate prior to the thirty-six-hour plane trip home.

Mrs. Remmington died less than a month later, not even living the full four months predicted by her own doctor, which of course, was dependent on his treatment. Because of her faith in a man who totally fabricated her treatment, Mrs. R. spent her final days sick and alone in a Third World country, enduring a grueling travel schedule that would have exhausted even a healthy person. And tragically she had the added burden of knowing she'd been swindled by a ruthless con artist when she could have used that time putting her affairs in order, conversing with loved ones or penning her memoirs.

What really happened? Using a false finger available from any magic shop, the doctor concealed a tiny container of blood. The doc then folded the skin back to make a crevice and dumped the blood on the patient, kneaded it around and then pushed his hand "into" the stomach simply by curving his fingers back out of sight. After dumping a clump of chicken entrails, he pulled it upward to show the malignancy being removed. The doctor didn't cure the patient, and he knew full well he didn't cure the patient. But then, dead clients give no references.

Pastors of Persuasion

There is something about the title *spiritual leader* that draws not only dedicated men of God, but those who seek to mooch off of rather than minister to their followers. Of all the cons perpetrated by man, I personally think leading them spiritually astray is perhaps the cruelest hoax of all. Were I in charge, these people would cause quite a holdup in the Pearly Gates Express Lane.

How the Mind Becomes Open to Suggestion

To understand the hold charismatic leaders have on their followers, I went to see Ken Steinmetz, a certified hypnotherapist, operating Hypnosis for Health in San Francisco. Steinmetz, who uses the technique to help people relax, lose weight and quit smoking, described hypnosis as that zoned-out state that comes about while performing repetitive tasks such as driving. In fact, the term *highway hypnosis* was coined to depict that experience of "waking up" in the driveway without the foggiest memory of the journey. While in this spontaneous trance, Steinmetz says we operate on automatic pilot from our *habit center*, a condition that renders us so open to suggestion that a radio advertisement can cause our car to swerve right into the nearest fast-food restaurant.

Likewise, we experience the same sort of spontaneous trance when we attend a lecture or watch TV, again causing our emotions to rise vulnerably to the surface, rendering us relaxed and open to exploring new ideas.

Groupthink

In George Orwell's bestseller *1984*, the author coined the term *groupthink* to define the us-and-them dynamic that takes place within a pack mentality. It's not always, says Steinmetz, "us *against* them," as Christians maintain themselves to be different from unrepentant sinners but not to actually hate them. Used positively, like-mindedness can bind football players into a cohesive team or, as in a situation like TV's hit show, *M*A*S*H**, give a group of doctors the kind of camaraderie that got them through the Korean War. But what often happens, Steinmetz warns, is that a society bound together by a lofty goal can become so determined to preserve the group's specialness that members sacrifice their own individual morality. Example: Political cover-ups.

Charismatic leaders promote this need to belong by using *projection*, a natural psychological defense mechanism that transfers their flock's negative self-images onto those outside the group. We're saved, they're doomed. We're righteous, they're sinners. We're white with shaved heads, they're not. This is exactly how Hitler was able to promote his master-race doctrine to the point of almost annihilating an entire ethnic strain. Such occurrences thankfully are rare, but groupthink is frequently used on a less grand scale to coerce followers into self-destructive behavior such as serving their leaders at their own expense. Says Steinmetz succinctly, "God has designed a check-and-balance system for his ardent promoters, and it's called *money*."

Other Controlling Techniques

Steinmetz says he personally thinks most spiritual leaders did not set out to con and swindle; they merely took advantage once they realized how much power they came to wield. Here are some characteristics that promote a destructive cult/groupthink scenario.

- **Isolation.** The group is segregated from society, including former friends and family, leaving very little room for reality testing.

- **Elitism.** The group professes a special message or esoteric knowledge that further sets it apart. The leaders are self-professed higher beings, surrounded by a circle of fanatics. Their appearances are planned and controlled.

- **Expulsion of dissent.** There is no tolerance for healthy dissent. Those who question find themselves shunned, denounced, spied on or even expelled.

- **Repetition.** Doctrines are reinforced repeatedly. Often the leader's name or some phrase is chanted to that end.

- **Rituals.** Strict behaviors, dietary restrictions, dress codes, speech patterns, gang colors, special languages or words are used to limit the members' free expression and individualism.

- **Urgency.** Very often cults promote an apocalyptic end-of-the-world prophecy that puts a deadline to their mission.

- **Fatigue.** Rigid schedules or long work hours create sleep deprivation, rendering members even more vulnerable to suggestion.

Spiritual Leaders

The epitome of con artists, Jim and Tammy Faye Baker simply *talked* and people sent them money. They said they were going to use it to help terminally ill kids and provide followers with condos at their Christian-based theme park, but instead they spent it on an air-conditioned habitat for their perspiring pooch. And mascara. Lots of mascara.

And then there was Jimmy Swaggart. Although he escaped the kind of charges that sent Jim Baker to the Big House, this conman spent much of his followers' contributions on visits to New Orleans's hookertown. Which is probably not how they intended their money to be spent.

And let's not forget Bhagwan Shree Rajneesh who recruited illegal immigrants and the homeless to strengthen his political following in the bucolic burg of Antelope, Oregon. In a case of the conned conning the conner, these habitat-challenged people kindly thanked their sponsor for the complimentary cross-country trek, but respectfully declined to convert. In the end, the government deported Rajneesh and seized his 64,000-acre ranch, applying the sale of it and other monies to the estimated $35 million in back taxes and other debts he owed.

In groupthink at its worst, charismatic leaders like Jim Jones and Reverend Sun Moon actually come to believe in their own divinity. Whether their credentials are actually earned or simply purchased via mail order, these particular charlatans have, simply put, come to believe their own press. And all together now, what do we call a person who spouts one philosophy and lives another? That's right. A con artist.

Faith Healing

In his revivals in the late 1980s, Peter Popoff called out names of folks from the audience, recited their afflictions and even spewed forth their doctors' names. He claimed he could accomplish this very impressive feat because he was in direct communication with God. Actually, it was his wife, Elizabeth, backstage whom he was in direct communication with—via a small receiver in his ear. And she was in direct communication with the prayer cards audience members filled out on their arrival.

Robert A. Steiner, in his book *Don't Get Taken!*, talks of assisting James Randi (The Amazing Randi) in busting a 1986 Popoff Crusade in Anaheim, California. Randi somehow managed to get the whole Mama/Papa Popoff communique on audiotape as Papa "healed" Virgil Jorgenson of his crippling arthritis.

Except arthritic Virgil Jorgenson was also alcoholic Tom Hendrys at a previous revival, who was also prostate cancer victim Abel McMinn and, before that, was also ailing Bernice Manicoff, a uterine cancer sufferer. Popoff "cured" Don Henvick in all these guises of all these nonexistent diseases.

Grifting the Grieving

This group of scams is distinguishable by the particular vulnerability of the victim rather than the credentials of the perp: a childless couple looking to adopt, an elderly couple facing decisions about their time left on earth, a child whose pet has run away. These small-minded perps propel their bunco on a very personal basis.

Adoption Scams

An adoption scam is a simple con with heartbreakingly cruel ramifications. A middle-aged childless couple places an ad looking to adopt, having been unsuccessful with the mainstream agencies. A pregnant woman responds, saying she's unable to keep the child. If they will just pay her medical expenses, the kid is theirs. After forking over $5,000, they discover on the eve of her due date that the lady has disappeared.

What's really happening? Sometimes the pregnant mom changes her mind. Other times, she simply isn't pregnant. Or perhaps she never intended to give up her child and just wanted somebody else to foot the bill.

Bail Bond Scheme

Late at night the phone rings, and a raspy voice asks the elderly woman, "Do you know who this is?"

"My grandson Larry?" the elder inquires.

"That's right," says Raspy. Quickly, the phone is turned over to the attorney who's been assigned to deal with Larry's troubles for his part in a fatal car crash. Calling from the police station, he says the kid needs bail money and he'll be right over to pick up all the cash she has. And please don't tell his mom.

What's really happening? Larry's home in bed, she filled in too many blanks, and these people are lying.

Hispanic Heist

The phone rings. Maria Hernandez answers and finds herself talking to a Texas priest who's calling for her cousin, Jorge. But Cousin Jorge is in Mexico, she informs the man of the cloth.

Not anymore, says the priest. Jorge swam to freedom and now needs $300, which the church will use to provide him with the proper immigration papers. Maria asks to speak with Jorge, but his swim-induced laryngitis prevents that. Noting her skepticism, the priest describes her cousin perfectly, right down to the scar that runs from his cauliflower ear down to the heel of his left club foot.

Convinced the priest knows her cousin, Maria's only problem is that it's 7 P.M. and the post office is closed. She promises to consult her hubby who's due home soon and mail off the loot tomorrow, but Father Bunk insists it must be done tonight. Luckily he has a nationwide listing of Western Unions and has located one in Maria's own hometown. And so the lady wires her ATM limit into Lone Star oblivion. She never hears from the priest or Cousin Jorge again, and when she calls back the 800 number, she finds it disconnected.

What's really happening? The "priest" is in cahoots with a Mexican connection, providing information about people down there who have relatives up here. Family-oriented Hispanic immigrants are the targets of this scam. For it to work, the transaction must be completed quickly, before Maria can track down her husband or mention the problem to others in her community, many of whom have also been scammed.

Bible Bunco

As made memorable in the movie *Paper Moon*, shortly after the death of a loved one, a package arrives COD. It's the Good Book the deceased has lovingly ordered for his adoring soon-to-be widow. Because Bubba was a coldhearted atheist who was illiterate to boot, his widow is especially touched and pays the hefty charges.

What's really happening? The scammerman's not illiterate, and his favorite reading source is the local obits.

Heirs on Demand

One day our soon-to-be client received a call from a Mr. Cox, an "heir finder," who asked as many questions about our future client's deceased mother as he seemed to have answers. He knew, for example, that Mom was a Russian-born orphan who'd shipped in from Shanghai in 1951 and ended up on welfare. He also insisted she'd arrived with an aunt and uncle and they all went to live in San Francisco's Russian community, a fact that belied our client's knowledge of her own family history. After peppering her with this quasi-accurate research, he dropped the bomb. She and her siblings had $609,874.19 coming to them from an unnamed inheritance, and he wanted half as a finder's fee for alerting them to their newfound wealth.

They didn't have to pay him until they got their money, as is standard in the heir-finding biz. But what wasn't standard was Cox's cut. He was to get half, and the six kids were to split the other half. Cox was insistent; they *all* sign, or no deal. Three immediately agreed, but the remaining sibs attempted to negotiate Cox down.

Then came the deadline, a common denominator in all scams. Cox insisted he had bigger fish to fry and couldn't be bothered with them anymore. Either they all sign or they could just forget it. The family continued to string him along, but secretly they hired the Rat Dog Dick Detective Agency to find the money for them.

It was a perplexing case, to say the least. Cox's story had several legitimate factors: The heir-finding business worked roughly as he claimed, with investigators such as himself taking the initiative in finding people owed money and then hoping they'd later pay for the service. The monies traditionally came from a variety of sources: Unclaimed Fund indexes, Public Guardian files, HUD refunds, forgotten bank accounts, etc. But if my clients were really the recipients of such monies, I couldn't imagine they wouldn't be getting calls from heir finders galore.

My first step, then, was to trace their mother's lineage, starting with the alleged aunt and uncle. The ship's alphabetized passenger list showed everyone's assigned number upon debarkation. By researching the numbers before and after Mom's—figuring a fifteen-year-old orphan would be disembarking with whatever family she had when arriving in a new country—we found a widowed woman with a child in front, and a boy of sixteen behind. As for the address Cox had quoted, it turned out to have been assigned to roughly a third of the arriving immigrants, and was the church that had sponsored the refugees.

Finding no evidence of a relative anywhere, I finally chose to investigate Mr. Cox instead. This grammar-school graduate who claimed operatives all over the world continued to work out of his inner-city property, as evidenced when he sleepily answered his business phone at 3 A.M. Also curious was the fact that if Cox didn't ante up $469 in property taxes within weeks, he'd lose that property altogether. A curious stance for a man who refused to budge from his 50 percent finder's fee.

The break came after the client recognized the names preceding their mother's on the passenger list as the alleged aunt and uncle. The problem was, unless eleven hundred people disembarked alphabetically, this couple was standing two hundred folks away from her when they got off the ship. I researched them anyway and found the retired janitor gent had died in 1972, his wife following in 1988. Their unassuming estate went to their daughter, Tossie Bledsoe.

Knowing my client's next question would be, "What about Tossie?" I proceeded to track her down, and unbelievably discovered that not only was she deceased, as well, but her estate came to exactly $609,874.19!

Unfortunately, the family proved to be no relation to Ms. Bledsoe. A very competent private investigator had already found Tossie's relatives in Siberia and was tirelessly working to have the money transferred there. Mr. Cox didn't toil nearly so laboriously. What was now perfectly obvious was that when the heir finder couldn't find any authentic descendants to present for the lady's estate, in order to collect his finder's fee, he simply chose to invent some.

LET THE BUYER BEWARE

"One ringy dingy!"

—Ernestine, when
asked how a
telephone scam
begins

In order for a con to work, it has to look like something else. As we've seen with the pigeon drop, it often looks like free money. In the section entitled "Pastors of Persuasion," we saw how it can masquerade as religion. With a sweetheart scam, it is made to look like love. But, perhaps the number one thing a con resembles is a simple sales transaction.

Why? Primarily because they are relatively inexpensive to pull off, both in terms of human and financial outlay. Not only does it come with the built-in justification "Nothing personal! Simply business!", it also is almost always mistaken for a simple bad investment, rather than what it often is—downright fraud.

Direct-Mail Malfeasance

In perhaps the most impersonal arena of all, direct-mail marketers simply produce the perfect pitch letter, buy a mailing list, send out their offering and wait for the cash to roll in. They never have to consider the feelings of their victims, let alone listen to the hardships imposed by the money they lost. A 1992 poll conducted by the National Consumers League/ Reference Point Foundation determined that 92 percent of all Americans had received "guaranteed prize" postcard schemes in the mail; 29 percent of them bit; 69 percent of those received no prize; and 91 percent of those couldn't get their money back.

The entire direct-mail industry, legit or not, is built on fulfilling a customer's order, as the product is described upon a page. An honest company will send along their good stuff and honor their money-back guarantee for any dissatisfied customer. A dishonest company might also send out a product, but it will be inferior to what was represented, and should the customer attempt to return it, he might very well find the 800 number disconnected and the post office box a dead end.

Now, here's the rub. Since no government entity has dared define *quality*, let alone *worth it*, the lines dividing a disappointing product and downright fraud are blurry, to say the least. By pushing the misrepresentation envelope, most direct-mail companies can operate legally, albeit immorally, while taking victims for a healthy chunk of change, check by staggering check. That doesn't mean this isn't fraud. It just means there isn't much anybody can do about it.

The Design

One way marketers mislead is to shift the emphasis. What the customer *could* win is declared in BIG BOLD LET-TERS while the odds of that happening are in lowercased 2 pt. faint gray type. Another tactic is to mimic a government or well-known entity by deliberately copying its style and even logo. If a disclaimer is there at all, no matter how small, this isn't even illegal. There is no law governing perception.

The Offerings

Legitimate mail-order companies offer catalogs and stay in business for decades. Since they have so much invested in up-front costs—design, production, the gathering of products—they need to build a loyal following to achieve success. Naughty firms tend to put forth a single product per mailing, which involves very little overhead. They have no need (or hope) of return business.

Telephone Trickery

Telemarketing fraud is estimated to cost consumers over $40 billion per year, $50 million of which is committed by Canadian perps who rely on jurisdictional complications to avoid prosecution. Whether Canadian or American, these ruthless telesharks peddle products that simply do not live up to their hype.

Tele-Untruth Central

Florida be thy name. What is it is about the Sunshine State that scoundrels find so winsome? They have a large elderly snowbird population, plenty of transient labor and an abundance of drug and other violent crimes to amuse the authorities elsewhere. In addition, Florida's rogue-friendly laws effectively protect assets of judgment debtors, were it ever to come to that, plus there is easy access to the Cayman Islands' confidential financial institutions. If scoundrels find the humidity too high to live in Florida, they might prefer residing in Texas, Arizona or California.

The Boiler Room

This is the heart of a teleshark's operation. It consists of a large arena of desks and a bank of phones, as well as folks who spend all day calling and/or being called by mooches from all over the country. In this hyped-up environment, any number of nationwide targets can be hit in record time. Because the official address is a post office box, there is no need for a fancy office, fine clothing or credentials. Should midnight flight become appropriate, business need not even be interrupted.

The Pitch

Telesharks love to rattle off standard scripts without waiting for a response. To win bogus prizes like boats, trips or jewelry, marks must purchase even more worthless items like pens, vitamins or jewelry. In addition, they are often told they must prepay taxes, shipping and handling charges, and/ or transfer fees. Telesharks have a pat answer for every objection. Easy touches make the infamous *suckers list*, meaning they are recontacted and/or their names sold to other boiler-room operators.

Ingredients of the Pitch

Some or all of the following will present themselves in almost every telemarketing pitch.

- The pigeon has been specifically chosen to receive an incredible offer of a vacation, prize or "free" gift, or in an investment scheme, a guaranteed quick profit is promised, with little or no risk.

- There will be half-truths mingled with downright lies. The target will recognize what he knows to be true and so accept the rubbish, as well.

- The oral representation will contradict the written contract. Follow-up material will disclose additional terms, conditions and costs—if any information is sent at all.

- There will be high-pressure tactics, often in the form of a time limit. The pigeon is asked to send money, give a credit card or bank account number, or have a check picked up by courier before he can carefully consider the offer.

- It's a deal. Whether the offer is an investment package or vacation, the pigeon is led to believe he will financially benefit somehow.

- The pigeon is assured there's no need to check with his attorney, family, local consumer protection agency, district attorney or Better Business Bureau.

The Perps

One reformed telescammer described many of his former colleagues as drug addicts who were able to read people like a psychiatrist and gear their pitch to the personalized needs of their victims. These boiler-room "yacks," he claimed, earn up to $100,000 annually with proper sales ability and experience. In *Flimflam Man*, author M. Allen Henderson describes the yack like this:

> As Ned gives you his oil-lease pitch, he paces back and forth, phone receiver clamped to his bare shoulder, hands jammed under his armpits, and waves his elbows up and down in a sort of frantic chicken imitation. This is called "flapping" in boiler-room lingo. Because phone solicitors, or "yacks," are thought to be most effective when they are both tired and excited, they frequently indulge in this exercise to get their blood pressure up. Coffee and cigarettes are popular among yacks because caffeine and nicotine enhance the hectic pace of the boiler-room environment. Although Ned sounds as if he should be wearing a suit and tie, he is casually attired in cut-off jeans and shower thongs. All around him other yacks, both men and women, are engaged in phone conversations similar to the one you are hearing.

Henderson goes on to describe how the manager will bound into the room in full gorilla-costume regalia, shrieking and beating his chest in order to increase productivity by getting the yacks all hyped up. Bells ring whenever another sucker bites the dust and periodically a yack will go into the hall for a cocaine break. There they discuss the *mooches* (suckers) and *laydowns* (mooches who bit right away) to whom they have just sold some *goat pasture* (worthless mineral rights). Henderson explains how the caller is kept unaware of this commotion, because the yacks are equipped with *confidencers*, which eliminate all background noise. I suspect some psychology is at work here, as well. That constant involvement in the overwhelming environment keeps yacks from getting drawn into the personality and problems of the person they are taking advantage of.

The Classic Cons

Mail and telephone schemes are often interchangeable. How the pigeon is contacted is immaterial—the bottom line is they are being had.

Sweepstakes Stings

Jeannette got a call informing her she'd won a $100,000 sweepstakes she didn't even remember entering. The caller said check number 43227 was sitting right in front of him and would be sent by UPS or FedEx as soon as she mailed off the 7 percent advance fee. When she told him she didn't have $7,000, he asked how much she did have. Thinking it wasn't any of his business, Jeannette quoted a very low figure. He then said the least they could take was $2,500. Had Jeannette fallen for this, she might just as well have burned the money in her fireplace. At least she'd have saved the postage.

Another bunco bit are those calls claiming to be the Publishers Clearing House Sweepstakes, that thoroughly legitimate company famous for its Super Bowl bust-ins on blue-haired old ladies. The senior is told Ed McMahon is going to deliver the prize himself and even take them to lunch! Then comes the proviso—the prepayment of federal taxes amounting to between $20,000 and $270,000, depending entirely on the yack's perception of the pigeon's ability to pay.

What's really happening? In April of 1997, Alisa Daniele Viarengo of Holyoke, Massachusetts, pleaded guilty to conspiracy to commit wire fraud for impersonating the famous outfit (a clue might have been that Ed McMahon represents American Family Publishers). Within a year's time, she and her cohorts had defrauded over a million bucks from elderly victims in eight states by collecting up-front taxes on prizes they never won.

Guaranteed Prize Scam

Mary called my chief investigator, Ann Flaherty, so excited because she could finally do something nice in return for all the kindness Ann had shown her in the past. She presented my pal with the brochure of a car she'd won—although she had to pay $29.95 for delivery, of course—which she intended to present to our nonprofit group, Elder-Angels, which ironically was formed to protect victims of financial fraud. It was only as we began to scour the fine print (eager to see just how they'd worm their way out of this one) that we realized it was a model car. Yes, a teeny little Ford Explorer, one thirty-second the size of Ford's real Explorer.

Soon after, Ann happened to discover all the prize redemption mail her elder had received in just the last week. There were at least twenty similar offers, and unbelievably, many of the return addresses were sequential post office boxes. Having fallen for a jumble of contests, awards and prizes over the years, this poor woman had so endeared herself to one twenty-eight-year-old superscammer that she was now a valued member of his sucker list. In fact, he was targeting her from no less than twelve separate companies, routinely selling her a variety of worthless products, sweepstakes and come-ons.

Contest Cons

Pushing aside the usual bills, the pigeon sees a letter claiming she's got a $20,000 check set aside for her from a sweepstakes she's entered. Not recalling the raffle, she dials the 900 number anyway and takes the simple "skill-testing" quiz necessary to claim her bounty. Eight minutes into the call, she's informed she's been disqualified because she missed calling by the deadline. Disappointed, she hangs up. Then comes the $55 phone bill.

What's really happening? The letters are always mailed on the eve of the expiration date. Or the simple skill test ain't so simple, after all. Or the fine print states the payoff might be as low as $1.37, but it's so teeny that an ant with an electronic microscope would need reading glasses to decipher it.

Recovery Scams

In this secondary scam, another teleshark telephones a victim of one of the scams above, telling her he can help her recover her losses. There is, of course, an advance fee for this service.

Travel Scams

A postcard arrives stating, "You have been specially selected to win a free trip!" When the pigeon calls the toll-free number for details, he finds a credit card number is required to hold the reservation. What's really happening? The free trip never comes up in conversation, but the deal seems so good, many bite anyway. Unfortunately, the only bargain here is the basement they call accommodations.

Unclaimed Funds Scam

The first big unclaimed funds scam began in 1866 and went on for nearly seventy years. The Baker Estate Swindle gleaned millions of dollars from over three thousand investors—all named Baker, Becker or Barker—when William Cameron Marrow Smith and others convinced folks to contribute "legal fees" that would return the center of Philadelphia to its rightful owners, that is Jacob Baker's heirs. Since the land consisted of Independence Hall, the Pennsylvania Railroad Station, Ben Franklin's grave and the Liberty Bell, many Bakers were more than willing to help wrest the land back from a dogged and nameless probate court.

One lone postal inspector, Alfred T. Hawksworth, spent twenty years gathering evidence before felling Smith and twenty-eight of his cohorts. Never accused of being a quitter, the seventy-year-old Smith was still working from his cell to continue freeing Philadelphia when he died in 1936.

Unclaimed Funds Offerings Today

Ironically, the average unclaimed funds proposal looks like a scam but actually isn't. In every state, there exists a microfiche of people who are owed money—from forgotten bank accounts, HUD refunds or whatever—and heir finders routinely scour these lists, separating out those folks due substantial sums, hoping the recipients will be so happy to have been found that they will pay their 25 percent to 50 percent fee. Since sometimes they do and sometimes they don't, on the whole it is the heir finder who takes the risk, not the client.

However, since people are becoming aware that these microfiches of free money exist, they are susceptible to the deals such as the single-offer mailing presented below.

IMPORTANT INFORMATION: Public Records indicate millions of dollars of Unclaimed Money have been turned over to the State of California for distribution.

Potentially $$$ of this fund belongs to you. Under California State Law Unclaimed Money MUST be returned to the rightful owner upon presentation of proper documentation.

For instructions and your *Unclaimed Money Collection Form* return this form along with a $10 check to: Unclaimed Assets. Make check payable to "UNCLAIMED ASSETS" and write [your reference number] on the face of the check. Your cancelled check is your receipt.

But what's really happening? What the postcard doesn't say is that the target is simply buying a letter telling him to go to the local library where he can view the microfiche. It doesn't say that many of the names come with no Social Security number or date of birth or any identifier, so the money is pretty near uncollectible. And they certainly don't mention that most accounts contain less than $50.

Slamming

Mrs. Brower is grocery shopping when her six-year-old spots a sweepstakes box offering a drawing for a shiny new convertible. She doesn't think twice about her child filling out the entry form and certainly never puts it together with the three-times-higher phone bill she receives a month later.

What's really happening? In May of 1997, Houston-based Brittan Communications International came under investigation by the California Public Utilities Commission for their practice of switching consumers' long-distance service without their knowledge or consent. BCI protested by claiming their "letter of authorization" was at the bottom of the sweepstakes entry form, and therefore they had not "slammed" anyone.

But PUC Special Agent Linda Woods argued that California law required companies to "thoroughly inform" their customers of the switch, and that the person who signed the card must be the customer of record and certainly not a child. BCI, says she, did none of these things and they are no longer able to perpetate this scam in California.

809 Numbers

Via a message on his voice mail, the target is told to phone about an emergency of some sort. After twenty minutes of waits, holds and transfers, he finally gives up, no longer buying the crisis yarn. Then comes the phone bill. He's been charged $25 per minute for the duration of the call.

What's really happening? Since 900 numbers are known to be charge calls, telephone scammers have moved out of the United States and into the Caribbean, where the area code is an unrecognizable 809, and the law allows them to charge anything they like for incoming calls. Now that the Caribbean has been divided into several area codes, the public is vulnerable every time they place a call to an area code they don't recognize.

800 to 900 Numbers

A wise mom and dad have used the phone company's "call blocking" feature to keep their teenage pervert from dialing 900 number sex lines. Still, when their phone bill arrives, they've been charged for such calls regardless. They complain but are told to pay up or be disconnected. What's really happening? Sex talk lines know concerned parents are thwarting their 900 number business, so they use an 800 number that rolls over to a 900 number.

Door-to-Door Duping

In the words of one convicted con artist, "Basically, anyone knocking on your door, forget it." The bottom line is, nowadays it's just not profitable for a legitimate business to make house calls. For the con artist, however, it's a different story. Because they have no money invested in product, they have no expenses either.

Charity or Religious Groups

These folks attack, and no amount of politeness will make the solicitors go away. What's really happening? Called *outsitting the customer*, the canvasser simply won't leave until he gets a donation of some kind. What the pigeon may never realize is that either the charity is completely fictitious or very little of the money actually reaches it. This is really just door-to-door begging.

City Inspector

An official says he needs to check the plumbing, furnace, heater, wiring, trees, whatever. There's always a problem and the service or appliance must be disconnected or replaced immediately. Not to worry, he has a friend who works fast and cheap. What's really happening? Fast maybe, but certainly not cheap. Not when you consider nothing's broken.

Product Demonstration

The solicitor offers to demonstrate his merchandise, and all the pigeon must do is sign a form proving to his boss the demo was made. What's really happening? The form is actually a contract, and when the stuff arrives, it's either overpriced or of inferior quality. Or both.

Retail Rip-Offs

Traditionally, retail establishments rip off the public less than their more mobile direct-mail and telemarketer cousins, simply because of the immobility factor. Still, they have their ways.

Bait and Switch

It was Knoxville, Tennessee, circa 1973, when a poor Appalachian woman came into town and, amid errand running, filled out an entry form to win a sewing machine. Then one day to her door came a gent in a Cadillac, with the little black thing under his arm. The sewing machine he carried was not the one she'd seen in the store, but something Betsy Ross might have used to whip up Old Glory. The woman had won second prize, the salesman proudly informed her.

With the twenty-year-old salesman was a young woman just out of college who was traveling around the country, working at odd jobs to support her wanderings. In this instance, she was training to sell sewing machines door-to-door in Appalachia, for which the company was paying her a whopping $100 per week. Though several years younger, the gent was her mentor.

When the young salesman presented the Appalachian woman with her prize, he kindly confided it wasn't really much of a trophy—only worth $25 and sure not to last— and proposed to her instead $100 off the first-prize machine offered in the raffle. What a bit of luck that he was the one to bring the prize, he informed her, rather than someone who played strictly by the book.

The young girl with him looked around uneasily. This was her third day of training, and although she'd seen unprecedented poverty, this backwoods family home was the worst. The house had two rooms, with walls constructed from layers of newspapers that had been treated against the rain. In these rooms lived Mom, Dad and their six children, one of whom was still in diapers. The forty-year-old woman was haggard and worn. Her husband was rawboned, his face black with mine soot and his hands calloused from hard labor.

The young salesman played the father like a fiddle. Although clearly the father couldn't afford the $300 sewing machine, the mentor appealed to his sense of honor involved in caring for his family. He pointed out how his lovely sixteen-year-old daughter could now make her own clothes, as well as the rest of the family's. Her eyes shone when she heard that. In the end, for the man not to buy the machine would have caused him to feel like a failure in front of his family.

The trainee had thus far been impressed with her tutor's glib gift of gab, but this last hour had been an embarrassment to everyone but the eager young salesman. Clearly, anyone could see it was not appropriate for this poor man to spend a penny on anything other than what went directly into his children's mouths. She shot her cohort dirty looks, but his only response was to back off from a sale he obviously wasn't making anyway and focus on selling the man a $200 machine instead.

After another hour, Dad finally caved and signed up for the "easy" payment plan. What he didn't know was that everyone who entered the contest won second prize, and because the little model was handmade, it actually cost far more to produce than the $300 model. There was great competition among the salesmen to peddle the top-of-the-liners, but if they couldn't, they were to somehow get out without having to "drop" the Betsy.

That was the last day the young woman worked for the company. Although she wouldn't hear the term *bait and switch* for many more years, she knew in her gut that her best-paying job ever—and for several more years to come— was simply immoral. After leaving the door-to-door sales, she went on to land a series of waitressing jobs before finally settling in San Francisco and becoming a private investigator and writer of a book on con games.

The Federal Trade Commission calls bait-and-switching, "An alluring but insincere offer to sell a product or service which the advertiser in truth does not intend or want to sell. Its purpose is to switch consumers from buying the advertised merchandise, in order to sell something else, usually at a higher price or on a basis more advantageous to the advertiser."

The Perpetual Going-Out-of-Business Sale

Once, on our way to lunch, I accompanied my consumer fraud investigator friend to an Oriental rug outlet that someone in her office noticed had been going out of business since the day after the earthquake. The big one. In 1906. Her assigned task was to cruise the store, take a quick count of the floor coverings, and then visit periodically to see if the stock was diminishing. Unfortunately, this chore was a tad more complicated than anticipated. The huge storefront was chockablock with exotic offerings, and the salesman informed us there was an entire warehouse to peruse if we failed to find something that struck our fancy there. Eventually, however, the store actually did go away, and so my pal never got the chance to say, "Up against the wall, you bait-and-switcher!"

INVESTMENT OPPORTUNISTS

"You knew I was a snake before you took me in."
—"The Snake," a
song by Al Wilson

And then, of course, there are the scams aimed at people whose goal it is to better themselves by investing what money they've already legitimately earned. Whether the investment be commodities, chain letters, distributorships or real estate, all that matters is that the pigeon has money that the scammer prefers to be his. Some of these endeavors can wipe out a victim completely.

Pyramid Schemes

Are we talking Amway here? Discovery Toys? Tupperware, for heaven's sake? Just what exactly are pyramid schemes, and how do they differ from that example of American ingenuity called multilevel marketing?

The thermometer the attorney general uses to determine the legitimacy of a multilevel marketing company is quite simply whether the profit comes from peddling the product or by selling the distributorships. The Federal Trade Commission insists there's no percentage requirement for this litmus test—a company is either legit or it's not. Tossing in a commodity to satisfy the Pyramid Police, they say, just doesn't wash. Bottom line, if a company depends on never-ending recruiting in order for people to make money, that firm is acting fraudulently.

Why would you want to write a book about a bunch of multilevel marketers? Might not. But the ramifications of a pyramid scheme can be so vast and devastating that it might just incite another unspeakable act—murder!

Ponzi's First Scheme

It all began in 1899 when a seventeen-year-old Italian immigrant named Bianchi sailed to America to seek his fortune. After failing at a series of honest and dishonest endeavors in Montreal and then bungling a people-smuggling attempt across the Canadian border, Bianchi decided to wipe the slate clean and start all over as Charles Ponzi in Beantown.

Now thirty-seven and working in an import-export brokerage house, Ponzi one day discovered that a postal reply coupon, which could be purchased for a penny in Italy, was redeemable in the United States for five cents. The coupon was intended to cover international return postage, but Ponzi had a better scheme. He prevailed on an overseas accomplice to buy the stickers en masse, which he then proceeded to sell at market value, a 500 percent markup.

So successful was his plan that he soon required more capital. Being the glib and persuasive fellow he was, Ponzi began collecting $50 from investors with the promise of returning to them $75 in three months' time. Small of stature but slick of tongue, Ponzi kept his scheme secret at the brokerage firm, but his reputation as a financial whiz was becoming legendary among his poor but honest tenement-dwelling neighbors. Ponzi even intimated Rockefeller was a client, although he declined to say which Rockefeller.

After Ponzi was canned from his job for not showing the proper remorse after coming in late one morning, his income became totally dependent on his new endeavor. But that was

OK because business was good. Virtually all his customers kept reinvesting their principal, which meant he had to fork out only their interest each month. And who wouldn't stick with the Ponz since he was returning a whopping 50 percent instead of the promised 25 percent on their investment.

One problem. Only so many international return postage coupons were issued each year, not nearly enough to satisfy Ponzi's eager investors. What to do! By now, potential funders were clamoring at the little Italian's door—but he had no product. Think our man Ponzi was going to tell them that? Well, then you just don't know Ponzi.

It wasn't long before the whiz kid figured out he didn't need product. Since nobody ever asked for their principal back, why not use the new investors' principal to pay back the interest of an existing investor? And so he did, a technique now known as *robbing Peter to pay Paul.* As they say in Italy, *no problema*, since there was no shortage of investors.

The pyramid business was booming. By 1919, wife Rose was working as her husband's secretary, plus he had a slew of clerks whose sole job it was to open the envelopes, record the dollar amount and then toss the bundles of cash into big wire baskets that Ponzi would then come around and collect. The sight of those brimming baskets of beautiful bucks sent investors scurrying into the streets in search of other funds to ferret out and entrust to their golden boy. Every evening, the happy Ponzis loaded the money into huge suitcases and carted it off to the bank.

Ponzi relocated to a posh mansion in Lexington but couldn't buy his way into high society. When his big bashes went attendeeless, he sent a fleet of taxis back to his old neighborhood to pick up his former cohorts, anxious to show his snooty neighbors that Italian immigrants, like blondes, sure knew how to have fun.

But society snubs were soon the least of Ponzi's problems. The press had started to take note, especially now that he'd bought up most of the Hanover Trust Company's stock, thereby gaining the controlling interest and becoming a millionaire ten times over. At first they reveled in the local immigrant-to-tycoon who had, indeed, found America to be the land of opportunity. Ponzi carried out the dream of many poor working slobs when he bought the J.P. Poole import-export brokerage firm for which he once worked, and fired the man who had fired him.

Boston was all atwitter with Ponzi fever, and everyone seemed to be either an investor or trying to scrape up enough money to become one. It literally took over the town at the beginning of the flapper era. There's no telling how long this happy life might have continued if that nasty press hadn't turned on him. OK, so all pyramid schemes are destined by their very nature to fail, but this was the first one and nobody really knew that. In any event, some hotshot reporter soon stumbled on Ponzi's Canadian criminal history, which caused some concern for investors, especially since the original scam was frighteningly similar to the one in which they'd invested. Politicians at first turned a blind eye—nobody wanted to be the guy who killed the golden goose—but the press was practically screaming for an audit and what could they do?

The constant media ragging finally wore down the public, and despite their good returns, many decided to withdraw their principal. Luckily, by now Ponzi had his own bank to turn to. He replaced its immense resources with personal IOUs and planned to invest the millions in another surefire moneymaking adventure. Gambling. Unfortunately, Ponzi wasn't very good at it. And so down came the Hanover Trust Company, along with a couple of affiliate financial institutions.

Oops.

In those days before pyramid scams were deemed illegal, all the authorities could get old Ponzi on was violating postal statutes, and then only because shortsighted Rose had notified investors by postcard that their interest was ready to be picked up. After that particular incarceration, he did some time for grand larceny, and then got deported back to Italy in 1934 at the age of fifty-two. By the time he sent for Rose, she had gone on with her life and was no longer interested. After attempting to blackmail the Bostonian officials who'd brought about his demise, and overseeing Latin Airlines in Rio de Janeiro for Mussolini, Ponzi lost his job, suffered a stroke and died in a charity ward at the age of sixty-seven.

Chain Letters

The most prevalent example of the Ponzi scheme today is the chain letter. "Don't break the chain. It's been around the world seven times. Bad luck if you do. Big bucks if you don't." In case you've never taken the time to read one, here's how it goes:

> Hi. My name is Connie Cahn, and a year ago my car had been repossessed, my home foreclosed on, and my name placed on a No-Can-Charge list at Bonwit Teller. In short, life sucked. TODAY, I'M ONE RICH MAMA!!!!!
>
> Why? you might ask. It's because I've made over $250,000 to date and expect to become a millionaire by the end of the year. Every time I go to my mailbox, I find CASH amounting to $600, $800, whatever. It's like Christmas, only better, because on Christmas all you get are socks.
>
> This money program works! In this perfectly legal business opportunity, you don't have to sell anything, talk to anyone or even leave home except to buy stamps and order more bubbles for your swimming pool.
>
> If you'd like to be like me, RICH RICH RICH, simply follow these instructions and in sixty days you should receive over $250,000 in cash! (Don't know if you've thought of this yet, but it's really easy to hide cash from the IRS!)
>
> Here are the steps:
>
> 1. Send $5 to each of the five names listed below. *Cash only.*
> 2. Remove the name at the top of the list, slide everyone up a spot, and add your name at the bottom.
> 3. Reproduce two hundred copies of the enclosed instructions, and order a list of 200 names from Names R Us, PO Box 001, Anytown, USA, for $26.

4. While waiting for your list to arrive, stuff and stamp those envelopes. *Do not put your return address on them.* (Going to jail for mail fraud will interfere with your vacation in the Seychelles.)

5. When your list arrives, stick the preglued names on the envelopes and shove them in the big blue box on the corner.

6. Run like hell, making sure the postman doesn't see you because even though this is *perfectly legal*, some mail-fraud officials don't think so.

7. Sit back and wait for your money to arrive. Given a mere 5 percent return, within sixty days, you should have at least $250,000 (tax free, of course) to spend on whatever you want!

OK, so let's say Patsy Pushover sends off two hundred letters and those people send off their two hundred letters, and so on and so forth through five generations, as is the plan. Assuming this incredible offer did sucker a whopping 5 percent of the recipients—five times what professionals consider a decent return—following the calculations through five generations would look like this:

1 person mails 200 pieces. 5% response = 10 people playing. **10 people mail 200 pieces** = 2,000 pieces out there. 5% response = 100 people playing. **100 people mail 200 pieces** = 20,000 pieces out there. 5% response = 1,000 people playing. **1,000 people mail 200 pieces** = 200,000 pieces out there. 5% response = 10,000 people playing. **10,000 people mail 200 pieces** = 2,000,000 pieces out there. 5% response = 100,000 people playing.

And how much would it be if a hundred thousand people all sent Patsy $5 in the mail? *Five hundred thousand dollars!!!* (Or in layman's terms, half a mil.) Wow!!! Zipperino!!!! But doesn't a hundred thousand people sound like an awful lot? Just to put this into perspective, this is as if the entire population of Bakersfield, California, responded to Patsy's chain letter. And I can tell you right now, there aren't a hundred thousand people that stupid in the whole of America, let alone in Bakersfield.

So if it is impossible to make money from chain letters, who are the brains behind this nutty endeavor, and more importantly, why are they doing this?

Not too hard to figure. Since the person at the top of the list is the only guy who's got any shot at making any money, you can bet your last five bucks, that's the confellow. Oh yeah, and see those other four names beneath? That's him as well. And, oh yeah, that Names R Us list you're asked to purchase? Yep. It's his.

And how much is he making? Well, if 1 percent—the industry standard—of his two hundred target market—each sent him $25 (two people times $5 for each of his five aliases) he'd make only $50. And if both of them bought his mailing list—undoubtedly comprised exclusively of other akas for himself—he'd make another $52. That's pretty pathetic when you consider the $64 in postage, along with photocopying charges, envelope prices, labor, etc. OK, so he's got a shot at second-, third-, fourth- and fifth-generation suckers, but chain letters traditionally peter out as they continue, not swell to include the entire population of Bakersfield. So if even the perp isn't making any money, why is he doing this?

Well, here's the punch line, folks. *It's because some other con artist has sold him this dumb idea!* Yes, it's true. As you will read in the chapter entitled "Biz-Op Scams," there exist confellows who sell "ideas" to aspiring entrepreneurs, not legitimate how-to books crafted by savvy professionals, but techniques so ill thought out they're destined to fail.

Big-Time Ponzi

In the late 1980s, FundAmerica offered its members discounts on long-distance calls, financial and travel services. But in actuality, the real product was "memberships," that is, the right to sell others the right to sell others. By the early nineties, FundAmerica had 90,000 salesfolks who'd bought up 800,000 distributorships from the corporate entity.

It wasn't long afterward that the cracks began showing. Bottom-rung investors might still be blaming their own sales abilities, but in reality only about 15 percent of the distributorships had been unloaded, and those mostly among the investors themselves. An outside audit showed only 6 percent of the sales force earned any commission at all, and out of those, four in five received less than $1,000.

Something had to give. And it did, in the form of the Florida state attorney general's office who, on July 19, 1990, charged FundAmerica, Inc., and its founder, Robert T. Edwards, with securities fraud. Following his arrest, confidence in the company understandably plummeted, and rather quickly, FundAmerica was thrown into bankruptcy. With "recovery room" antics, some high-ranking FundAmerica members formed a firm called Club America and targeted the victims, claiming they wanted to help them recoup their losses.

Beating the Heat

With pyramid schemes, the jurisdictional problems can complicate prosecution. Often two or more states need to act in concert to wipe out the offender, although one particularly aggressive attorney general can certainly cripple an enterprise.

Commodity Cons

Coins, gemstones, precious metals, art, oil and gas leases: These are the most common offerings in investment fraud. Citing current trade embargoes and world events, as well as the importance of certain metals to defense and high-tech industries, telemarketers, as always, urge clients to act quickly. In 1983 and 1992, the FTC brought suit against 325 fraudulent investment firms, winning judgments totalling almost $100 million. Alas, that amounted to a mere ten cents on the dollar in victim restitution, mostly because the defendants had already spent the profits.

Oil and Gas Lease Lotteries

Here's how this raffle legitimately works: For an entrance fee, plus a "delay rental fee" (which varies according to acreage), the lottery winner realizes the opportunity of leasing a property's mineral rights from the Bureau of Land Management (BLM), for $1 per acre per year. Of course, this parcel may not produce any oil—without drilling, there's no way of telling—but even so, an oil company will undoubtedly sublease this land at $100 per acre, plus pay 4 percent to 6 percent in royalties, just to find out. The worst that can happen is the investor will lose the lottery and forfeit the entry fee, since the delay rental charge must be returned to him.

With a scam, the investor is offered a surefire way to win the government lottery. As luck would have it, the telemarketer claims to have made a deal with the current administration to rig a certain number of leases so his customers can win.

What's really happening? Called the *Reagan Pitch*, for the first administration fingered as coconspirator, there simply is no such agreement. When the loser loses, the company closes up shop and skedaddles, never returning the delay rental fee as promised. It turns out, of the pigeon's $10,000 loss, only a third goes to pay the BLM's entry fee, 15 percent ends up in the salesperson's wallet, and the rest disappears with the skedaddler.

In the early eighties, one oil and gas company's owner was indicted for fraud after just sixty-six of his sixty-six thousand "guaranteed winners" won. One of their salesmen admitted to making $500,000 per year for your basic nine-to-five job. A firm called Westchase went so far as to sell investors land that wasn't even in the BLM lottery. (The government no longer holds these lotteries.)

Gold Investments

This highly esteemed metal is normally stoic against the fluctuation of the dollar, besides being considered a liquid investment, meaning it can quickly be turned back into cash.

Investors buy gold in many forms, but purchasing it in bullion is considered the safest. Unfortunately, a load of bullion can really weigh down a Pinto, besides being too bulky to hide under the bed. Since delivering this load by armored car and storing it in a secured facility can cut into the profits, most investors leave the commodity in the seller's possession and accept his negotiable warehouse receipt as legal tender— which it's universally considered to be. As an added incentive, telescammers often offer a "deferred-delivery commodity option," which will discount the purchase if delivery of the warehouse receipt is delayed by a mere ninety days.

What's the scam? Do I even have to say? In the early eighties, Bullion Reserve of North America sold $1 million worth of gold sixty-one times over, made possible because no one ever took possession of the gold. Ultimately, they were indicted for bilking over thirty-thousand clients.

Real Estate Rip-Offs

Since real property is an asset greatly coveted by Americans, con artists will always find a way to cash in on this dream.

Advance Fee Scheme

When Mr. Rolph needed a $4 million development loan, he turned to Illinois's Northern Mortgage Corporation, which represented itself as providing $50 million in monthly loans financed by highly rated bonds. To qualify, Mr. Rolph was required to pay 1 percent in advance fees, in this case $40,000, with the understanding that the fee would be refunded if the loan did not materialize.

What's really happening? Northern's sole source of revenue turned out to be the advance fees. Which, of course, were never refunded. All the marketing literature and letters of association turned out to be bogus, and by the time the FBI caught up with them, at least fifty victims had lost over $1 million.

Assessor's Kickback

The target receives an envelope from the "Real Estate Tax Review" with a red notice declaring, "Important Tax Information Enclosed." Beneath the embossed seal, the letter states, "Under Proposition 8, you are entitled to a temporary reduction in taxes when the market value of your property falls below the assessed value." Cool! Off goes the target's $65 fee in the next day's mail.

What's really happening? Note the letter does not state the homeowner is actually one of the overappraised, just that such a category exists. Also this information can be had for free, just by calling the assessor. Although the law requires direct mailers to officially state they're a private firm, there is no way of legislating graphics and perception. By incorporating official-looking seals onto letterheads and designing company names reminiscent of government entities, direct mailers deftly skirt these laws.

Home Equity Fraud

There are four basic types of home equity scams: caretaker cons, home improvement scams, refinancing schemes and equity purchaser fraud. The average victim is over seventy, African American and makes under $24,000 per year on a fixed income. Fifty percent are single women or widows.

Caretaker Cons

The elderly homeowner is courted by a new "friend" who persuades the senior into either signing over her deed or granting power of attorney. Once done, the friend takes out a loan on the property or sells it and keeps the profits.

Home Improvement Scam

An unscrupulous contractor induces the homeowner to sign a lien contract secured by the property. The work is then either performed shoddily or not at all. Either way, the contractor has what he wants: a promissory note allowing him to foreclose on the property if the homeowner misses just one payment.

Refinancing Schemes

The lender promises to lower the homeowner's debt — credit cards, car payment, mortgage, etc.—by consolidating all his obligations into one low monthly payment. But the resulting loan is designed to be more than what the homeowner can pay, so when he defaults, the lender can start foreclosure procedures immediately.

Equity Purchaser Fraud

The homeowner has already received a notice of default and so is susceptible to this "expert" willing to help him out. Unfortunately, the scammer just further encumbers the property or offers to purchase it for less than market value.

Part With Parcel

The call comes. You want to retire to Florida and here's your chance. With a price this low, how can you lose? What's really happening? Ever heard of the Everglades?

Rental Scams

All the good places list the same phone number to call. Thus enticed, the residentially challenged pays the deposit with the assurance it'll be refunded if they don't find lodging within six months. But after six weeks of hearing the apartment has just been rented or finding it not as advertised, they give up and find something else. When they ask for their deposit back, it's like talking to their newly leased brick wall.

What's really happening here? Los Angeles's Global Management went way beyond just misrepresenting their refund policy. Bunco investigators found they didn't even have an exclusive on the properties they were offering, and some property owners had never even heard of them, let alone signed a contract. Global just reworded existing classifieds, substituting their own telephone number.

Time-Shares

The target receives an offering of a free resort weekend, including airfare. To fulfill his end of the deal, the mooch suffers through a high-pressure sales pitch while folks around him scream, "Take my money!" He's informed of appreciating land values, the incredible area growth, and how he'll never have to fret about escalating hotel prices again. The mooch buys, sight unseen, and then realizes how far seventy miles from town really is, and what it's like to vacation in summertime Nevada when the swimming pool has not yet been built.

What's really happening? Traditionally these properties are so overpriced, they'd simply never sell if buyers took the time for comparison shopping. And those other couples so eager to buy? Singers.

Job Opportunities

There is, of course, a segment of the population who'd prefer a high-paying do-little job over the trouble of starting a business. For these folks, superscammers have a solution.

Exotic Work Elsewhere

The ad reads, "How to Get a $1,615-a-Week Job in Alaska Even If Totally Unskilled." Because the average Lower Forty-eighter knows nothing of Alaskan economy except that the wages are high enough to match the cost of living, this ad has quite a draw.

What's really happening? The ads misrepresent the number of jobs available, as well as the salaries. The warning signs are that having no skills is an admirable quality and that placement is guaranteed.

Mystery Shoppers

This is layman's terms for a "detective" who visits boutiques, bars and restaurants, surreptitiously checking to see if the clerks are properly ringing up the purchases. Now, who wouldn't like to be paid for spending money? And so the pigeon calls the 809 number. To the tune of $9.95. Per minute. Higher on weekends.

What's really happening? As mentioned in "Telephone Trickery," Caribbean countries—as denoted by the 809 area code and, of late, others, as well—are not governed by U.S. law and so can charge whatever they like for an incoming call. The Mystery Shopper Kit costs $89.95, but there are far more eager shoppers than stores that need snooping.

Out-of-Work Professionals

Via the Internet, recent college graduates are targeted by agencies offering to place them in their chosen careers for a finder's fee, kind of like headhunters in reverse. The luckiest of these grads are simply out the fee; others discover their personal financial information accessed and their bank accounts emptied or their credit ruined. Working with the FBI and postal inspectors, the FTC brought seven actions against nine such companies in 1997. Due to their efforts, more than $1 million was made in refunds and restitutions.

T W E L V E

BIZ-OP SCAMS

"Wherever there's an opportunity, there's an opportunist."
—Globe Magazine

Nobody outlines how to commit a swindle better than Bruce Easley in his frighteningly frank book *Biz-Op: How to Get Rich with "Business Opportunity" Frauds and Scams.* As entertaining as it is horrifying, this how-to primer gives step-by-step instructions on just how scoundrels can go about draining "mooches" (his word, not mine) of their hard-earned bucks by taking advantage of the fact that they want to go into business for themselves. Easley's premise is based on luring sincere investors into bogus "business opportunities," which rather than propelling them along a new career path instead thoroughly alleviate them of their nest eggs. In 1997, the Federal Trade Commission determined Americans reported a whopping $250 million lost to biz-op scams.

The Players

When a scam is as complex as a pay phone scheme, it can provide jobs for several suspects, as defined below.

The Scammer

This is the guy who runs the ad and then supplies the turnkey kit to the investor. He's also a flat-out liar, knowing full well no money can be made from his ill-conceived enterprise.

The Locator

This fellow places vending machines or charity boxes in the "strategic locations" guaranteed to bring results. Locators are, of course, shills, working with the scammer to string investors along until all the cash is collected. The more creative ones will do anything to place a box, from wearing an eye patch while peddling for the National Federation of the Blind, to taking out a vending machine they placed for yesterday's client, in order to accommodate today's.

The Singer

These phony references substantiate the opportunist's claims by impersonating satisfied customers. Paid by the call, these phone pals read from a script, reciting how much they made and how hard they don't have to work to get it. Carefully prepped, a singer knows the complete breakdown of each item: cost, retail value, the store's percentage and, of course, the net profit.

The Mooch

Although this might not be insider lingo for the victim, *mooch* is what Bruce Easley calls the aspiring entrepreneur, and I've continued to use it because it emphasizes the opportunist's perception of the victim. The mooch is not, as you might expect, the person who buys the end product, but the guy who purchases the product in hopes of reselling it. Stay-at-home mooches are called *bon-bon eaters*.

The Deal

There are nine components present in almost every biz-op scheme. These carefully thought-out hooks make it almost impossible for the mooch to locate his tormentor once the sting is complete.

1. **The Advertisement.** Most biz-op scams are offered via the classifieds found in legitimate publications like local papers and supermarket tabloids. Folks assume since the periodical is trustworthy, so are its advertisers. But most publications have absolutely no interest in verifying their advertisers' claims, since doing so might lose them revenue and gain them nothing. For their part, scoundrels learned long ago it was easier to pull an ad than to manage a midnight move to Tucumcari.

   A typical advertising cycle runs three weeks—just long enough for the pigeon to receive their shoddy merchandise and call about their money-back guarantee.

2. **The Address.** The mail drop looks like a street number but acts like a brick wall.

3. **The 800 Number.** The phone is always answered by a service or voice mail, since the opportunist has no desire to speak to anyone who has actually already invested in his product. The toll-free number not only disguises his location, it captures the mooch's phone number, as well. Best of all, it's easily disconnected, acting as a dead end to bad sports and pigeons with temper.

4. **The Offer.** Typically biz-op scams are no-brainer turn-key operations offering a 20 percent to 30 percent profit for an under-$15,000 investment. Added incentives are the ability to work at home, flexible hours and a be-your-own-boss environment.

5. **The Guarantee.** Routinely a thirty-day money-back-refund is offered. Yeah, like you can find them in thirty days.

6. **The Endorsements.** The references are actually singers, paid for every call they take from a would-be mooch.

7. **The Product.** Most companies actually send the merchandise, since not doing so would constitute outright fraud. And, after all, it's not like the product is worth very much.

8. **The Payment.** Cashier's check or COD. Rarely are

credit cards accepted since (1) only companies with proven financial histories qualify for merchant accounts, and (2) even if they had one, their account would be debited every time a customer returned the merchandise. Which would be a lot.

9. **The Delivery.** Everything comes FedEx, of course. Mail fraud is such a hassle.

The Bottom Line

Since the mooch knows very little about the field in which he has chosen to invest, when his new business fails, he routinely blames himself. Should he actually consider litigation, he'd have to serve a defendant he can't find, across state lines, for a few thousand dollars. And then collect? I don't think so.

The Come-Ons

In his book *How to Recognize and Avoid Scams, Swindles, and Rip-Offs*, Graham M. Mott lists these common phrases that suggest a scam is in the offing:

- Do you want to be rich and famous?
- Six-figure income.
- Earn $100,000.
- Earn $10,000 per month.
- Financial freedom.
- Make over $___ per hour or $___ per day.
- No selling required.
- Ground-floor opportunity.
- Moneymaker.
- Money machine.
- Easy money.
- Incredible profits.
- 500 percent profit.
- Earn ___ percent, guaranteed.

- No-risk investment.
- No investment required.
- Start without any capital.
- No inventory necessary.
- Low overhead or no overhead.
- Incredible overrides or residuals.
- Complete, full or 100 percent corporate training, support or backup.
- Your cost as little as $____.
- Ongoing repeat business.
- If you want to make a lot of money or get rich, call us now.
- Unlimited earnings.
- You can easily become a millionaire.
- I started my own business for only $____.
- Marketing breakthrough.
- Products at below wholesale prices.
- How to become wealthy or grow rich.
- How to make a financial killing.
- Turn your spare hours into big income.
- How to make big money at home.
- Deal direct, no middleman, keep all profits.
- Special introductory offer or limited-time offer.
- Hurry or you will miss out.
- Be financially independent.
- The safest opportunity of the 1990s.
- Chance of a lifetime.
- Too good to pass up.
- Protected territories available.
- I guarantee you will make $____ or I'll double your money back.
- Income day one or first-day profits.

- You have won one of three fantastic gifts.
- To receive your free prize, hurry and call 1-900-XXX-XXXX.

The Pitch

There is a direct correlation between the number of phone calls involved in a pitch and the amount of money the investor is expected to spend. With a generic stuffing-envelope scam, it's a one-shot deal. For the more financially demanding scams, there are usually at least four phone calls.

1. During the first call the object is to get the mooch to accept the scammer's FedEx package. To accomplish this, the scammer goes for the greed factor, emphasizing how much money the investor will make.
2. The second call is the *singer set-up*. The mooch is encouraged to call the phony references.
3. An urgent call is made after the singers report back about whether the mooch is "hot to trot" or still debating. Now, the scammer claims someone else is interested in his territory, so he must act quickly. If the mooch still insists on procrastinating, the opportunist gives him two days and then launches into . . .
4. The *close*. The mooch is strongly encouraged to overnight a cashier's check immediately.

The Scams

Biz-op scams fall into two categories. The more ambitious moncymaking projects, such as vending machines and pay phones, are targeted at investors/mooches with at least a couple of thousand dollars to invest. Traditionally, mooches tend to be upwardly mobile couples who've saved their earnings and are now looking to either retire or supplement this income with a part-time no-brainer.

Then there are the low-investment, income-producing cons like envelope stuffing and charity honor boxes, which appeal to stay-at-home moms, the disabled and folks with small aspirations and low self-esteem.

At-Home Assembly

"Turn your home into a small factory and become rich," reads the ad in a tabloid or romance magazine. "Assemble our devices at home. We pay up to $1,000 weekly. No experience. Send S.A.S.E." What's really happening? Mom pays $200 for $20 worth of jewelry she can't possibly assemble in the time given to fulfill the contract.

Charity Boxes

This con appeals to stay-at-home moms who need a little extra cash. The ad suggests she can make $1,000 per week while working out of her house and setting her own hours. Further, she'll have no overhead and will even enjoy "huge tax advantages."

All Mom has to do is replenish charity boxes already placed in her neighborhood, and then send the charity $2 each month per box. She can keep the rest. Unfortunately, the teleshark tells her, they've already found someone for that cushy job, but they have a limited number of contracts to place more boxes.

Mom is urged to act immediately, and she does. Her $100 kit includes the contracts, boxes and the phone number of a "locator" who knows the best places to leave the containers. Mom buys fifty charity boxes at $2 each.

The boxes do come, but the containers are far cheesier than Mom expects. In fact, they're simply cardboard boxes with holes for the Tootsie Pops and a slot for the coins. But now that she's invested, what is she to do? When Mom goes to collect, she can't even find the first box until the manager fishes it out from under the counter, explaining it took up too much space. At the second location, she's told the locator simply dumped it there and left, and there is no room for it. In those locations where the boxes are still in operation, the take is pitifully small, certainly not worth the drive across town.

Mom blames herself. She can never do anything right. She avoids talking about her new career, hoping her husband will forget she invested in such nonsense. When she calls to invoke her money-back guarantee, she's told that because she missed her weekly report, the offer is no longer valid. By the time the first monthly payment is due the charity, Mom's given up on her new business venture altogether.

What's really happening? Mom's promised return was grossly exaggerated. What she didn't know is that most charities are delighted when people elect to collect money for them, and hand out their contracts freely.

Stuffing Envelopes

The scam that advertises "Earn $1,000 per week stuffing a thousand envelopes!" works only on people who never stop to wonder why anyone would pay them $1 to put a piece of paper into an envelope when a direct-mail marketing firm would do it for less than a penny. What's really happening? After receiving the mooch's $35, the opportunist sends him a "kit," consisting of the following letter:

> Congratulations on your new envelope-stuffing career! With this letter you can make, as I do, $1000 per week. Simply run the following ad in your favorite newspaper:
>
> "MAKE $1,000 PER WEEK STUFFING ENVE-LOPES. SEND S.A.S.E. TO (Insert your name here.)"
>
> Then just wait for people to send you their $35, like you sent yours to me. When they do, simply send them a copy of the letter you are now holding. If you receive just thirty responses per week, you will make $1000. Good luck on your new envelope-stuffing venture!

Vending Machines

"Snack route opening up in hundreds of new locations. Earn up to $1,000 per week for as little as a $5,400 investment." Snack vending machine scams work along the same principle as charity honor boxes; they sell the mooch an "established" route that simply won't produce the revenue promised.

As a bonus scam, the disheartened investor is often contacted by "another" outfit, wanting to take his vending machines off his hands—at a fraction of their cost. Those machines are then supplied to subsequent mooches.

Distributorship

The ad says, "Are you familiar with Lancôme and Clinique? Well, now our research department has developed a product that is as good, if not better, than these esteemed brand names. After years of European research, we are finally bringing our merchandise to the U.S. and are looking for distributors interested in placing them in fine department stores."

What's really happening? The third-rate merchandise (usually cosmetics or greeting cards) is bought in bulk at government auctions for pennies each. Fine department stores are not interested in this junk, because regardless of the quality, without name recognition it's worthless. And the "brand-name illusion" the mooch fell for doesn't impress sophisticated department store buyers. Now the pigeon finds the only way to unload the stuff is the same way he bought it, sight unseen.

Pay Phones Scams

Dave and Glennis responded to an ad in their local newspaper that encouraged them to make $35,000 per year by investing in fourteen strategically placed pay phones. They did everything right. They contacted the Better Business Bureau, who had no complaints listed against "Statewide Bell." They called the Vending Association of North America (VANA), who declared them a member in good standing, and even the three references the company provided reported that the return on their investment exceeded their wildest expectations.

Dave and Glennis bit—to the tune of $15,000. While Statewide was "completing the paperwork," an independent locator went about finding locations for their phones. Statewide even dispensed programming instructions; however, the couple was advised to wait until they had all the locations before beginning that complicated procedure. Then Dave called the company's 800 number and found it "temporarily disconnected." He "FedExed " them a letter—using Statewide's account number—and FedEx phoned back to say the company had moved, left no forwarding address, and their account was "not billable at this time."

We found Statewide Bell was on their third such incarnation in the pay phone business. Their profits thus far: $2.5 million. They always fled the coop in that window of time between accepting the investor's dollars and when the phones were due for delivery. Their latest landlord had been stiffed, as well, but he happened to know they'd relocated just down the street. And although the U.S. Postal Inspector was hot on their trail, the slothlike local officials allowed them to continue to operate—and accept money—while the authorities made their cases.

A variation on this theme substitutes public fax machines for pay phones.

Franchise Fraud

Traditionally, there are three ways to venture into the business world: Start your own company, buy an existing one, or invest in a prototype that the investor then runs himself. In general, franchises are considered far less risky than starting from scratch—mainly because the distributor has alleviated the guesswork by investigating the demographics and supplying a quality product.

But, once again, wherever there is an opportunity, there's an opportunist. And so quasi-promoters use this American dream to unload ill-conceived enterprises destined to flop. By the time they do, the promoter has quietly gone out of business, leaving no assets to collect, should the plaintiff bother to sue. Had the investor been a tad more astute, he might have questioned the lack of Fatty Arburgers franchises already on the street, as well as the fact that the distributor was more interested in selling his distributorship than in the product it offered.

GLAMOUR SCAMS

"You oughta be in pictures."

I think it's an American curse that most of us think we are special. I don't see Sherpas in Tibet with this particular affliction—not that I've had a lot of in-depth conversations with Sherpas—but in my daily job of answering phone calls from all kinds of people from all over the nation, if there is one common thread, it is that everyone believes themselves to be superior to the majority of the population in some way. Sometimes it's their looks, other times their perceived sex appeal (often in obvious defiance of their looks), and other times it is their real or imagined talent for acting, writing, painting or banging on the drums. And because people are so susceptible to flattery, there exists an entire industry made up of scam artists whose sole goal is to fleece the flatterable.

Show Business

In showbiz, a good many of the scams happening today are not technically illegal, just impossibly immoral. And as with other con artists, glamour scammers have no need to risk jail terms when they can get the same results by coloring just inside the lines. But as Ed Hooks, actor/teacher/author and columnist of *Callboard* magazine's "Inside the Industry" column, says, "Whenever there is a business where people have unreachable hopes and dreams, you will find someone who will promise them those dreams will be fulfilled."

The victims of these scams, says Hooks, are frequently good-hearted dreamers who want to become stars. Real actors are not usually ripped off, because they attend classes, talk to other actors and generally have a feel for what's happening in the industry.

The Casting Couch

They've got a name for it. Sexual harassment. And a law against it. But nowadays blatant propositions are rare. According to Hooks, it's much more likely for a producer to simply ask for a "date" rather than request the ingenue sign the contract in the buff. But several years ago there was a "big Hollywood agent" who clearly stepped over the line. He would bring actresses into his office to read scenes, with himself as the other actor. He would get them involved playing a love scene and then decide it was time to test their improvisational skills. It was hard to deny the charges when his self-produced sex tapes surfaced in the courtroom. And, yes, he went to jail.

Talent-Finders

There are only three categories of legitimate talent facilitators in Hollywood—casting directors, talent agents and managers. Prevailing state law insists all three must make their income solely from actors' commissions rather than by charging the client upfront for services. When they commence casting, producers and directors either call an actor's agent or ask a casting director to set up a cattle call. That's how the business works. Period.

But the "talent finder" creates the perception of a job that just doesn't exist in Hollywood by misrepresenting themselves to be the liaison linking talent and agent. To do this, they sponsor talent searches and sell acting classes and pictures to naive hopefuls. But since the talent finder's income comes directly from charging the client, according to California law they are operating illegally. "Talent finders have no legitimate function in the business," says Hooks succinctly. "Nobody in Hollywood is looking to them for product."

The Cyberspace Connection

Still, they flourish, in part thanks to the Internet. Hooks says, yes, the Internet *is* the wave of the future, and it's only a matter of time before producers and directors discover the ease and immediacy with which they can peruse talent via this medium. But, says he, it's simply not happening yet. In fact, most of the production hierarchy don't even own computers, says Hooks. (Yes, I am writing this in 1997.)

Cyberspace talent finders promise aspiring actors that by plastering their head shots all over the Web, they can have a presence in Hollywood even if they live in Poughkeepsie. These amateurs work from the privacy of their own homes, putting forth splashy Web pages that make them appear quite the corporate entity.

This medium's anonymousness makes it a no-man's land sure to be abused. Clients can be solicited from across international borders, providing scammers with unlimited access to pigeons, and because the scam crosses state lines, there are jurisdictional problems, as well. In the end, "actors" who don't know better can spend hundreds of dollars per year for virtually no exposure in Hollywood.

Making Movies

Frank Maddox is the fictional name of former pro football player, former sports announcer, and B-movie star. (No, he's not the one who killed his wife so civilly.) This Frank Maddox, circa 1985, had gone into producing action movies, which consisted, as far as I could determine, entirely of collecting venture capital from well-heeled investors who were anxious to be associated with the glamour of Hollywood.

My client was just such a fellow. He gave Frank Maddox $250,000, and although he never met the man, he stayed at Frank's home while the flashy guy was out of town. Sure, savvy investors know the movie business is speculative, but my client never even considered that the movie might not be made. After all, he "knew" Frank. He'd seen his sports commentary on television, caught his photo spread in *Ebony* magazine, watched a bit of Frank's short-lived TV show, and even bought the vermouth he touted from high up on those Sunset Boulevard billboards. Still, as far as I could determine, the single effort Frank put forth to produce the film was to place a blurb in *Variety,* announcing it was so. In fact, my research showed a series of such proclamations over the years, all for movies Frank had never made.

When our bad boy never even sent a thank-you note for the loot, it was cause for my client's worry. When he no longer responded to his phone calls, it was cause for concern. But when Frank didn't show up in court, it was downright infuriating. Unopposed, my client got a $300,000 judgment—the loan, interest and attorney's fees.

I figured collecting the default judgment would be a snap. I found Frank had a Jaguar, a home near Mulholland Drive, enough rare coins to start his own small country, a vineyard in Napa and, of course, the income from being on all those billboards. It wasn't even a particularly hard job. All these assets were listed in his recent divorce, a split from the very same woman he was married to as he posed as a beauty-draped bachelor in the *Ebony* spread.

Once Frank saw that a couple of his favorite toys had been attached, his attorney sprang into action, pleading before the court that ignoring this irksome suit was not Frank's fault, but a consequence of his own negligence. Could he have another chance? OK, said the judge. In the end, Frank's shyster made life so expensive and unbearable for my client, he finally decided just to cut his losses and move on with his life.

Reviewing Movies

At the other end of the spectrum, we have the more modest investor, who also wants to be associated with the movies. And possibly Heather Locklear, if that could be arranged.

And so, he answers an ad in his local newspaper that claims to be looking for people to review movies. Only after the sucker has shelled out $24 for the proper forms (the money will allegedly be refunded to him after he files eight acceptable movie reviews) does he learn the evaluations are to be eighteen pages long, handwritten on legal-size yellow pads with a no. 2 pencil, and that he must finance the return postage himself. Four months after this five-hour ordeal, the victim is informed his review was illegible and therefore unacceptable.

Publishing

First, let's talk about how publishing legitimately works. At the top of the food chain are the Random House people and their cronies. When they accept a manuscript, they give the writer an advance on royalties, which means they predict how many copies will be sold, and advance the writer some healthy portion of their first commissions. As a courtesy, they also provide the writer with however many free copies for family and friends to find fault with.

Next there's the self-publisher. Here the writer produces his manuscript on his own desktop-publishing program, contracts with a printer, and then arranges for distributorship, either personally or through a rep. For writers who have a niche book not of interest to a large publisher, this is a viable option. I have even done it, and quite successfully.

And then there is vanity publishing—which is where the scam comes in. Here the con artist misrepresents himself to be a "publisher," but one who looks to the author for financing. Writers who don't know about the book business don't realize that books don't get sold without a distributor, and since these folks have no distribution network, there's not a shot in heck they are going to sell any copies. In a true scam, the vanity publisher offers to store the books for the writer, and then prints only a hundred or so of the five thousand copies the writer paid for. Unless he sells that first hundred himself and needs more, he will never know.

Health and Beauty Bunco

Virtually anyone who cares about their fitness and good looks is susceptible to the kind of false advertising the FDA was created to regulate. Our drug and health-food counters are full of nonprescription "natural" remedies that may or may not do little or nothing. Companies are now required to be less vague in their claims, but many, always anxious to present their product in the best possible light and always pushing the envelope, are not going voluntarily into that still night.

Snake Oil

The term conjures up Wild West quacks who peddled old-time concoctions like Kickapoo Oil, Swamp Root, Indian Cough Cure, Autumn Leaf Extract for Females, Ocean Weed Heart Remedy and Prompt Parilla Liver Pills at carnivals and county fairs. In the 1905 *Swamp-Root Almanac*, one tonic was advertised as "a great kidney, liver and bladder remedy" and recommended to everyone—even those who felt perfectly fine. Stressing that "thousands have kidney trouble and don't know it," the ad listed fifty-six common symptoms of Just Plain Living that pretty much put their target audience at a whopping 100 percent.

Kickapoo Oil was the brainchild of two Wild West showmen who peddled their wares from brightly colored horse-drawn wagons until 1880. "A quick cure for all kinds of pain, good for man or beast" was their call until the FDA said "No can do." After the FDA insisted on truth in advertising, their product was more modestly labeled, "for aches and pains." Sales dropped off substantially, and now it's nearly impossible to find a bottle of Kickapoo Oil anywhere.

The Mark Eden Empire

For nearly two decades—the 1960s and 1970s—Eileen and Jack Feather promoted their body-enhancing products through advertisements in women's magazines and tabloids. They promised to turn women into Barbies (out with the bust and in with the thighs), and hopefuls shelled out $40 million. But after sixteen years of dogged pursuit by U.S. Postal Service lawyer, Tom Ziebarth, the body-beautiful bunco bums finally agreed to settle out of court for $1.1 million. That left them with only $38.9 mil. Poor babies.

Mark Eden's most popular product was the Bust Developer. Ads used to state, "Add up to three inches the first week or your money back." But after a highly promoted and equally entertaining water displacement test performed on thirty-four well-endowed University of Arizona coeds in a tub of H_2O, the USPS Consumer Protection Division fined Mark Eden over $1.1 million and made them stop advertising their product. They didn't much care, since by that time they'd made a fortune off flat-chested women everywhere.

Another product they advertised was the Thigh Reducer. This, of course, appealed to every woman. The Mark Eden company also promoted Slim Skins, which converted one's own household vacuum cleaner into an "exciting and effective" inch-reducing machine. The postal inspector didn't like these products much either. And neither did his fat-thighed, small-busted wife.

Electronic Gadgets

I don't even want to talk about this one. I have, somewhere in my closet, a $150 battery-run gizmo that is supposed to zap away arthritis. Not that I have arthritis, but I do have a face that needs lifting, and it promised to do that, as well. The doohickey, when activated, presents a gentle buzz that does nothing but remind me what a doofus I am.

Natural Birth Control Pills

In advertisements in *Mothering* magazine in 1977, women were told that by taking eight pills at once, they'd be pregnancy free for six months. It didn't work for eighty-six surprised new mamas-to-be, including two on the staff of *Mothering* magazine.

Sex Enhancers

One company, now defunct, twisted a Navy study regarding the role of zinc deficiency in the diet of malnutritioned boys to proclaim that their own NSP-270—when taken three times a day and with food—would produce better erections. The postal authorities decided food alone would do the same trick and put an end to this nonsense in the late eighties.

Diet Patch

In the midnineties, full-page ads ran in national tabloids promoting a patch that, when placed on the body, sped up metabolism and burned up fat. OK, I wanted to believe, and it even made a bit of sense since quit-smoking patches work on basically the same principle—by dispensing some miracle medicine directly into the bloodstream. But I'd learned my lesson with the $150 battery-run gizmo that hadn't perceptively lifted my face as yet, and so I remained patch free.

To free myself of this spell, I wrote an "Ask Rat Dog" column on the matter, which forced me to research their claims. This is what I learned:

- The report on which the product's credibility was based had been published in "one of America's largest national magazines," yet they declined to name that periodical. If it was a legitimate study in a recognized medical journal, would they not have named it?

- The study was performed by "a research company," which the fine print revealed to be their own. And it wasn't a medical investigation but a marketing survey.

- The main ingredient, "fucus," was described as "a natural algae containing very high levels of 'certain ingredients'." Fucus, along with its certain ingredients, was completely unknown to Dr. Dean Edell, San Francisco's own TV doc/medical reporter, even though it was boasted as being "recommended by many physicians."

Medical Alert Firms

In 1997, Smart Medical Alert Systems of Pompano Beach telemarketed the over-seventy crowd, many of whom took the product just to get the pesky peddlers off the phone. (Ever heard of hanging up?) Customers were told the initial service was free and, after that, was cancelable at any time, but the small print contradicted their claims. The actual contract limited the cancellation period to seventy-two hours and required certified notification as well. One elderly victim endured a nine-hour sales pitch—some things I can't explain—and another found a $2,485 one-time charge on his credit card bill rather than the $38 per month he'd agreed to. The Florida attorney general put the kibosh on that firm, as well.

F O U R T E E N

GENUINE IMPOSTORS

"The Postman Always Rings Twice."
—James M. Cain

("Except the first one wasn't really the postman.")
—Me

OK, in all cons there's a bit of bulldozing going on, but this chapter is all about those scams in which the victim turns over an asset solely because of the confellow's credentials. With impostor gags, scammers portray themselves as something they're not—an official of some sort, a celebrity perhaps, even a member of law enforcement—to get what they want: money, or freebies, or even just a measure of control.

Of course, you'll want your characters to fall for the gag—and the readers, as well—and not discover they've been had, right up until the second body comes tumbling off the roof. But whether your impostor is the perp, the victim, or even the heat, here is how real con artists pull off their shenanigans.

The Classics

Bank examiner scams, 911s, badge plays—these classic cons go hand in hand with pigeon drops and handkerchief switches (see "Classic Street Cons") and are often pulled on the same victim, once she proves herself scamworthy. The prey log in at 60 percent women, 40 percent men, simply because those are the statistics of people still alive at the preferred victim's advanced age. As for the perps, they're normally a highly efficient team of traveling criminals with no redeeming social value whatsoever.

The Bank Examiner's Scam

In this con, there are commonly three perps. The *phone man* uses his gift of gab to convincingly portray an authority figure. The *pickup man* is the only person the victim ever sees and the guy who gets the money. And often there is a *lookout man*, as well, who accompanies the victim to the bank, insuring that if anything suspicious goes down, the gang can pull a successful getaway.

Normally the mark is contacted by phone, chosen for an old-fashioned name like Ida, Henrietta, Maude or Gertrude, or gleaned via their husband's obit. This is one of the few cons that play not on the victim's greed but on their willingness to help humanity.

The following is an actual victim's statement taken in July of 1994. The victim's name has been changed to Mrs. XXX due to pigeon privacy laws.

This morning about 11:45, I answered my phone to have a man's voice say, "Mrs. XXX, I'm a bank examiner at the bank," which meant to me, First National, as that is the only bank I do business with. He went on to say, "We are conducting an investigation about a problem here in several accounts where customers are having money stolen from their accounts, one of them from your savings account." I said, "My goodness, that's a surprise. How much have I lost?" The reply was $3,600. I said, "That much? How could I have such a loss and not know it?" He hastily went off on a different tack. "We at the bank do not generally enlist the aid of a customer but since you are one of the victims, we hope you would be able to help us out and cooperate with us on solving this case." I said, "Well, maybe I could help, what do you want me to do?" "We would like you to draw out some money for us and take it to where our representative will pick it up. We are setting it up to be put in a 'dead account' until the problem is solved. The bank is standing behind this and you will not lose anything."

All this time the man had not given his name, so I asked him to spell his name for me. He said he was Mr. Sanders, but it was pronounced "Saunders." He told me then what they wanted me to do but I mustn't talk about it to anyone, especially anyone at the bank until they could solve their problem. He wanted me to go to ZZZ, the bank branch there, being where I did most of my banking, draw out $3,600 in $100 bills, being careful not to count the bills myself, let the clerk handle the bills and put them in the envelope. Then take them to JCPenney's back door, park as close as possible and in a few minutes a Mr. King would come to the car, that I need not get out at all, then I was to go straight home and he would call me there, to give me my next move. All this time, I thought I was doing this for the bank, helping them solve their difficulty, and get my money back. I seemed to have been in a trance state, because I did everything I was told to do, as if I was their robot! Didn't have a single thought that this was a scam.

I got to the bank about ten of 1:00 P.M. The clerk, whom I know well, asked me if I was buying something special with all that money and I said no, it was for an emergency. Then she said, "You be careful with all that money in your purse." And I really wanted to go back and tell her what was being asked of me, but I had told them I wouldn't say anything because I might keep them from catching the thieves. I had asked earlier how I was to know Mr. King, would he have a badge or identification pin on him? Mr. Sanders said I didn't have to know Mr. King, he would know me. This was a suspicion but it did not make me alarmed. Mr. King showed himself within five minutes after I got parked, picked up the money and told me to go straight home and Mr. Sanders would call me. I had barely gotten in the house when Mr. Sanders called and said, "You made it back in record time." Then I said, "What do you want me to do next? I'm getting tired and I need to have my lunch." Mr. Sanders said, "Have your lunch and I'll call you back in ten minutes." I had my lunch and in ten minutes, Mr. Sanders called and said they (me thinking "they" was the bank) wanted me to draw $3,000 out of my checking account and take it back to JCPenney's and this same Mr. King would pick it up.

About this time I was sort of coming out of my trance, or stupor or whatever I was in. I clearly wasn't using my brains. I had doubt about taking money from my checking account, but I did, still thinking the money would go into this dead account and be returned to me. You have no idea what a smooth spiel this Mr. Sanders gave in his authoritative voice. So, I took the $3,000 back to Penney's and in a short time, the same Mr. King came to the car. I had a good look at him this time. He was tall, at least six feet, slender, clean shaven and a short man's haircut. Wore a dark suit (blue) and had brownish hair and wore glasses. The frames were large round ones, bigger than most. Mr. King told me to return home and Mr. Sanders would call me. So, I discovered when he called Mr. Sanders that we finished this part in good time and they thought that they had almost solved the case but felt there might be one more to round up and close the case. Thanked me for my help and said they would have to wrap the case by Friday and he would call on Friday to tell me how it all worked out.

I was slowly coming to realize this was not what it seemed. I knew I should call the police or the bank but didn't on the slim chance it might be on the up-and-up. After dinner, I called my daughter in Maryland and she said, "Mother, you've been conned out of your money, kiss it good-bye." Call the police (sic), but I was too tired from all the activity and now that I knew it was a complete scam, I had to deal with my pride and my anger at having been so thoroughly duped. Up to now, I had considered myself lucky to have kept so well and right-minded until my eighty-fifth birthday. Now I am grateful for my good health, but I'm annoyed that my angel on my shoulder took the day off when I needed her the most.

911/Bank Examiner's Scam

According to the National Association of Bunco Investigators' Jon Grow, this variation on a theme is the hottest ticket in town right now. In fact, even as I was interviewing him, they were tracking one gang from Harrisburg, Pennsylvania to Frederick, Maryland, to Reading, Ohio. Grow personally knows of over $750,000 gone to bank examiner scams in the last six years, and since most of these crimes aren't reported, who knows how much really has been lost?

The con goes like this. An elderly woman gets a call saying the chief of police—whose name she recognizes—needs to speak to her, and she's to call him back immediately on 911. The woman picks up and redials, and the dispatcher says, "Anytown PD." The elder asks for the chief and is connected.

The chief then proceeds to inform her that somebody at the bank is fooling with the accounts, and since she's one of the victims, he needs her help. She's to withdraw $9,000 in currency, take it to a nearby strip mall and wait in her car for the detective. Between them, they devise a code word so she'll be certain she's giving the money to the right person.

The woman does as she's told. A plainclothesman approaches her from the rear, flashes a badge, mouths the code word and takes the money. As soon as she's home and in the door, the chief's back on the phone telling her there's been a problem. Either the bank's security camera wasn't working, or there was an additional teller involved or whatever. She needs to do the whole thing again. And so she does.

What's really happening? The 911 illusion was created by the crooks never hanging up after they called her the first time. When she supposedly redialed, she was actually just picking up on the already connected connection. About the only time an elder fell for this gag and lived to laugh about it was when one old gent took his money directly to the police station rather than wait for the detective in the parking lot.

Badge Scam

In 1986 when Jon Grow was a detective sergeant with the Baltimore PD, he got a call from a local bank saying one of their elderly patrons was attempting to withdraw $10,000 so she could participate in what they recognized as a pigeon drop. Now, naturally, customers have full access to their funds at any time, but in this pre-privacy-mad era, this particular financial institution went the extra mile to protect their patrons and took such liberties as calling the police. When the *drag broads*, (lady perps) saw the bank manager questioning the *shaky mom*, (old lady susceptible to enemy do-gooders) they split.

Sergeant Grow took her statement and made a point of explaining that on the heels of a pigeon drop often comes another scam called the badge play. This second set of suspects portrays themselves as the PO-lese (which is how Jon pronounces it) and pulls the kind of con as described in the story above. Grow emphasized that he and Danny will be the only cops working on her case and that if she's contacted by any other police, she should call them.

Six weeks later, the old woman is back in the bank attempting to withdraw $16,000 because her nephew is "in a Virginia jail." This time the clerk can't talk her out of it, and then—ta da!—suddenly the computers go down and the old woman has to come back the next day in order to withdraw the funds. Grow's detectives Danny and Paul go "scooting up," and the two crooks outside again take off.

So Grow calls the victim and says, "Mrs. XXX, you remember me? You met me down at the PO-lese station. You know those two guys in the bank? Well, they're with me. They're the real PO-lese. And those two other guys? They're the phony PO-lese." Still, he couldn't shake her. She just had to have the money.

The next day at noon, the woman called Grow and fessed up. These were not the only two times she'd withdrawn funds from the bank. Just after the first thwarted pigeon drop, she'd gotten a call from a "captain," saying he was sending over two detectives. As he was speaking to her, sure enough, they knocked on the door. They told her there was a problem with her currency, so she showed them the $10,000 she kept in a strongbox. They declared it "counterfeit" and seized it, informing her she was in a whole lot of trouble. Then they wanted to see her bankbooks, and so discovered her CD and savings account. The captain then informed her she needed to cash in the CD to cover the bad currency she had in her possession. Otherwise, they'd have to arrest her.

In the six weeks between her talks with Grow, the suspects took the victim to the bank six times, totalling her loss at $44,000. Finally she sat down with Grow's book of usual suspects and, coming across Oscar Thrash's photo, exclaimed, "That's him! That's that Sergeant Thomas!" When Grow said, "We have warrants for him," she said, "You mean he's not the real police?"

A week later, Grow had already locked up the local driver and issued arrest warrants for the others. Then the woman called to say the crooks were back. Grow gave her the usual precautions and started "hooting and scooting" to get the surveillance in order so he could nab the suspects in the act. Ten minutes later, she called back, asking, "Are you sure there isn't a Sergeant Thomas and a Sergeant Smith?" It seems the conmen had noted her new hesitant nature and figured she might be in contact with the real cops. So they called her right back and, upon finding the line busy, kept trying until they finally got through. When they did, they reamed her for dealing with the "downtown police" when they were the "real police."

Oscar Thrash ended up with fourteen years in prison. Well, actually seven with probation and all.

Variations on a Theme

Sometimes the faux cops tell the victim the suspect has just written a check for $40,000 on her account. Since the check hasn't yet cleared, she needs to get her money out before it does. Or they tell the victim they've caught the thieves and retrieved her stolen funds, *however*, since it has proved to be counterfeit, they are going to lock her up unless it's replaced.

Why This Works

It took a while for Jon Grow to figure out why badge scams are so successful. He notes that after a pigeon drop, very few victims want to accept they've been duped. They want to blame someone else, and 80 percent of them name the bank teller since this is the last person they had contact with before they lost their money. So when the phony cops come along and confirm the bank teller was involved—even showing Polaroids of their cohorts in mug shot tradition— the victim is more than eager to transfer the blame.

Nigerian Letter Scam

This con has become so prolific, it's practically a classic. And unbelievably, the perps are not even physically located in this country.

It goes like this: Some Nigerian official, for example, the Group Managing Director of the Nigerian National Petroleum Corporation and a member of an ad hoc committee set up by the federal government of Nigeria to review contracts awarded by the past military administration between 1985-1993—writes to the head honcho of a small business stating he's got $25 million and change that's looking for a home in an American bank account such as his own. Chosen for his fine reputation, for this awful inconvenience the businessperson will receive 25 percent, which is a whole lot of couscous in any country.

All that's necessary on the part of the businessman is to supply the company's name, address and where to send the money, that is, their bank account number. What's to lose, some silly pigeons might think, since the worst that can happen is that they won't get the $25 mil.

What's really happening? Well actually, the worst that can happen—and usually does—is that the pigeon will, after a flourish of intercontinental faxes and phone calls, actually pay the 1 percent tax—a mere $250,000—required to "release the funds," and then find the official has "died" and no one else knows anything about this. Another worst thing that can happen is that the Nigerian "official" will print his own checks for the account and/or use the letterhead to issue his own letters of recommendation or credit. But the very worst thing that can happen is that the mark will actually travel to Nigeria to consummate the deal and then get fleeced at the airport. The worst has in fact happened, and in such numbers that warning signs are now posted at most international airports counseling folks not to travel to Lagos, Nigeria.

Its Predecessor

The Spanish prisoner game dates back to 1588 when Philip II of Spain played war against England. In this version, the English mark was contacted by letter or in person with the message that a fellow countryman had been imprisoned in one of those awful sixteenth-century dungeons and required funds in order to bribe his captors or pay his ransom. It wasn't that the hapless hostage was without means—he was in fact quite wealthy— he just had no immediate access to his fortune. But, of course, once released he would be quite generous in sharing his massive wealth with the respected businessman willing to help him out of this unfortunate mess. For collateral, the courier offered a treasure map or other valuable papers, along with a rendering of the captive's lovely languishing daughter, who would also be most grateful—we're talking really grateful—for his release.

What's really happening? It's not that the prisoner isn't grateful. It's just that he's no prisoner. There is no daughter. If there is, she's no fox. Or she simply isn't *that* grateful.

Celebrity Cons

If one is going to go to all the trouble of impersonating someone, why not go for someone famous and well respected? Now you'd think people might notice, and although some surely do, apparently not enough to discourage the intrepid impersonator. In the midnineties, a New York fellow had some luck with his J.D. Salinger imitation, which worked chiefly because Salinger was such a recluse nobody knew what he looked like. His main take, as I recall, was gourmet food and some really fine wine.

River Phoenix

But New York City isn't the place bumpkins fall for the celebrity scam. Take the case of Lynn from Santa Cruz, California, who met a guy who told her he was River Phoenix. (This was before he died.) *Yeah*, she thought to herself, *he sort of looks like River Phoenix, but it's kind of hard to tell with the shaved head and all.* As a test, she asked him why, if he was a big movie star, he was homeless, to which he replied he hadn't been paid for his part in *My Own Private Idaho*.

Lynn's friends watched River Phoenix videos all that evening with the perp and then went to see *Sneakers*, which had just hit the theaters. He must have been a pretty close match, since her pals continued to invest in "River's" food, housing and carousing. Still, Lynn, being one smart cookie, had her doubts.

Before long, River wanted to move in. Even though she was ten years older and just a little bit desperate, the last thing Lynn needed was another dating mistake. She wrote the "Ask Rat Dog" column, inquiring how to determine if her new beau was really River Phoenix. I verified Phoenix had been paid for *My Own Private Idaho*, although it remained my opinion that he should not have been. I then kindly advised her that although I was sure she was charming and altogether fetching, what this homeless man no doubt really saw in her was simply that she lived indoors. At that time, the real River Phoenix already lived indoors—with a massage therapist in Florida.

Copper Con

Karen Shockley's first contact with seventeen-year-old Kevin Morse came when she was an officer with the California State Police and he was a cadet/explorer assisting at a DUI checkpoint. Bright and personable, he quizzed her as they went about arresting drunk drivers; he asked about her agency, how to apply, what kind of jobs were available, the testing process, etc. She gave him her business card, suggested he come on a ride-along and didn't think much more about it.

The next time Kevin's name surfaced, he'd gotten a citation at the State Building for parking in a police vehicle parking space. The office gossip had Kevin presenting to the sergeant on duty a homemade placard bearing the Office of Emergency Services emblem. This was a little silly since not only was the vehicle not a cop car, the plates were registered to Kevin's mother. The sergeant called OES and asked if Kevin worked there. Upon hearing he didn't, the sergeant let the citation stick.

Then Karen got an impersonating-a-police-officer case. She ran the plate, and when the Department of Motor Vehicles (DMV) sent along the driver's license photo, Karen said to herself, "I know this guy." She recognized him as the cadet/ explorer who'd quizzed her so thoroughly the year before.

According to the complainant, about 11 P.M., five teenagers had been stopped while returning from a fast-food joint near their home. It seems there was a half block where a neighborhood street was one-way, and they, as many residents do, scooted through rather than observe the law and take the block around. Well, out of a house came a guy in a California Division of Forestry volunteer shirt, complete with sleeve patch, gun belt and nightstick. He chased the car on foot until they stopped. Saying he was "like the CHP" (California Highway Patrol), he detained the occupants, informed them of the violation and even read their transgression from the code book. Moving to his house with the explanation that he was "running DMV checks," he threatened to take them to jail if they didn't cooperate. The driver asked if he could deliver the fast food back to the apartment, where one member of their party was waiting, and received permission to do so. But, Kevin warned, if he wasn't back in three minutes, he was carting his cronies off to jail. At the time, Kevin was nineteen years old and living with his parents.

After interviewing the complainants, Karen elected to do a *knock and talk*, police lingo for a friendly visit where the suspect will, in theory, voluntarily incriminate himself into the slammer. She awoke him at 7 A.M., the earliest allowable by law, and Kevin answered the door with a cheery, "Hi, Karen." The officer explained she was working on an impersonating-an-officer investigation, and Kevin invited her to sit with him at the kitchen table. Upon questioning, Kevin had an excuse or explanation for everything. Yes, he'd stopped the car, but no, he didn't imply he was with the CHP, nor any PD for that matter. Yes, he talked to the kids, but no, he didn't threaten or detain them. Karen asked if she could see the CDF volunteer shirt, and there in the left breast pocket (where police carry their little notebooks) was a 3" × 5" card with what looked suspiciously like driver's license numbers. Back at the office, Karen determined they were other victims of this same crime.

On the way out, Karen spotted Kevin's new, white Ford Tempo four-door—the exact model California government agencies employ. The vehicle had been backed into the driveway, so its rear bumper was not visible from the street, and stick-on lettering provided the vehicle with a phony unit number. All together, on or in the vehicle, Karen found two antennas, two red lights and one yellow, a scanner, a handheld microphone, two "Kojak" rotating lights, a trunk cell phone, a police baton, the infamous blue windbreaker, two CDF jackets, and a police wallet that holds a "flat badge." Things didn't look good for Kevin.

Officer Shockley then tracked down other possible victims, and sure enough, all said Kevin pulled them over for minor infractions—one because his radio was too loud—and brandished his law enforcement stature. Routinely, Kevin took their licenses to the trunk of his car and "ran" them for arrest warrants. When one fellow mentioned Kevin was carrying a .45 automatic handgun, Shockley knew he was clearly out of control.

Shockley obtained an arrest warrant and, because a gun was involved, a search warrant, as well. This time, her 7 A.M. knock was answered by Kevin's heartbroken parents who confided they always knew something like this would happen. They told of having to literally disown Kevin between ages twelve and fourteen because "he did everything he could to violate the family's moral standard." When Karen entered Kevin's room, she found it piled with so much stuff she had to walk on top of it to get to him. There was no way he could even sleep on the bed.

That was Karen's last face-to-face contact with Kevin, but she continued to get calls from other investigators regarding his bizarre behavior. Among other adventures, Kevin acquired a fire truck by applying for a government grant, claiming he and a business partner were going to provide security and fire patrol services to residents. Although anyone can own a fire truck, Kevin's had red lights and a siren, as well as an E-plate, denoting an emergency vehicle (which Karen got revoked due to his existing probation conditions). The grant stipulated the partners were to pay off the truck within two years, but since they never got any contracts, and because Kevin was in jail the day the loan came due, they eventually lost it.

Then a federal investigator called, challenging Kevin's claim on a government employment application that he'd never been arrested. And that led to Karen's discovery that Kevin now had himself a new, white four-door Crown Victoria, the exact model of CHP's unmarked patrol cars. Again, anyone can buy one of these—except that Kevin hadn't bought his. Instead, he'd procured it, along with four others, by submitting a carefully crafted purchase order to CHP headquarters in Sacramento.

And it wasn't over yet. Still in his early twenties, Kevin had managed to obtain a job that required a low-level security clearance at the San Jose airport, sitting just the other side of the metal detector, which apparently was as far into the airport as he was allowed to go. And yet he managed to find his way into the highest level of a security area, approach an airline crew and escort them onto the tarmac. One attendant became suspicious because instead of checking their credentials, he just strode up to them and said, "C'mon, let's go." When she quizzed him about the lack of procedure, Kevin replied, "I know who you are." When she asked to see *his* credentials, suddenly Kevin's imaginary beeper went off, and he said, "Oh, Alaska Airlines is paging me. I gotta go!"

That's certainly not the end of Kevin's story; it's just all that's been reported to Karen so far. Employing profiling techniques, one FBI expert predicted Kevin would go into corporate banking fraud, probably by his early thirties.

Various Short Cons

Most impostor scams are short cons, since it's only a matter of time before the victim discovers the fraud. Here are a few.

The Drop Box

In this gutsy maneuver, the con sets up a desk beside an ATM in a busy shopping mall, throws up an "out of order" sign and accepts merchants' deposits. In the 1980 bestseller *Catch Me If You Can*, Frank W. Abagnale Jr., con man extraordinaire, tells this and many other tales, each more amusing than the last. If you want to study a charming impostor up close, I highly recommend this book. I must admit I totally bought the book when it first came out, but upon this last reading, I began to think the author was conning me, Johnny Carson, and enough readers to make this book the bestseller it was. It matters not; true or false, it's one heck of a read.

The Little Boy Scam

In Salt Lake City in 1997, a thirteen-year-old boy gained widespread media exposure with his touching tale of how his parents abandoned him at a local bus stop. His call to social services sparked the media's attention, a torrent of public concern and at least fifty cash donations, as well as offers of places to stay. Two newspapers even set up a trust fund.

But the thirteen-year-old boy wasn't. Either. Instead she was Birdie Jo Hoaks, a twenty-five-year-old homeless woman who'd attempted the same scam in at least eleven other states. Ironically, it was the nationwide exposure that did her in. Vermont authorities recognized the case and called Utah to rat her out. When confronted, Birdie Jo admitted she'd made the whole thing up in order to find a warm place to stay. She did. Twenty-three days in the local jail.

COUNTERFEIT AND CREDENTIAL CONS

"Brother, can you spare a dime?"

Counterfeiting (the duplication of currency, personal and traveler's checks, credit and phone cards, and merchandise) and forgery (the alteration of original documents) are the forerunners of America's fastest growing crime, identity theft. Technically, these are just more impostor gags but here it's the prop that is the imitation, rather than the person.

Currency

Manufacturing one's own filthy lucre used to be quite the production with crooks spending big bucks, and legitimate ones at that, to produce bills that could pass for those coming from the Federal Reserve Bank. But with today's color printers and copiers, counterfeiting is easier than ever, says Dan Vaniman, a retired supervisor of the Secret Service, now with the Federal Reserve Bank of Miami. What the copiers can't reproduce, however, is the almost imperceptible security strip imbedded in the bill and the microprinting around the edge. But since few clerks know to watch for that, making one's own money demands just a couple of thousand dollars in start-up costs.

Phony Money

So how are phony bills spotted? One myth is that those inexpensive "counterfeit checking" pens sold at office supply stores will show up the phony goods. In actuality, since the ink reacts to the paper's chemical compound, the results vary tremendously. If the paper is similar to that supplied exclusively to the Federal Reserve Bank by Crane and Company, the pen simply won't note the difference. Vaniman puts its accuracy at about 50 percent.

How then is counterfeit money removed from the system? If a clerk suspects a bill, his option is to either refuse it or call the cops. The litmus test the police then use to determine if the customer is the duper or the dupee is based largely on whether that bill is the only counterfeit one in his possession.

Still, sooner or later, all lucre, filthy and otherwise, makes its way to a Federal Reserve Bank, where it is routinely tested. The FRB can tell which bank gave them the phony bill; however, the trail usually stops there. Vaniman says most crooks are caught via old-fashioned informants and surveillance. "We arrest a suspect, flip him around and send him back in," he says in cop talk. Then a surveillance is set up to catch the entire printing process in action. Right now, says Vaniman, San Francisco's United States Secret Service (USSS) field office has $26 million in their evidence vault, awaiting trial. I'd love to hear the defense on that one.

"Just for a point of info," says Vaniman, "about 90 percent of all counterfeit is seized by the USSS prior to its hitting the streets and the public being victimized."

Spotting a Counterfeit Bill

Let's face it, the new $100 bills just look phony. To determine if that's true, the American Bankers Association suggests noting these security features and how the bill reacts to simple tests:

- **Color-shifting ink.** Tilt the bill back and forth and watch the color of the number on the lower right-hand corner change from a distinct green to black and back again. If it doesn't, it's phony.

- **Watermark.** One of the first anticounterfeiting devices, an embedded watermark, visible when the bill is held up to the light, will appear identical when viewed from either the front or the back. On a counterfeit bill, it will be much more distinct from the front, because that's where it was printed.

- **Security thread.** This plastic strip runs from the top of the bill to the bottom, just left of the portrait, and in microprinting spells out "USA" or "The United States of America," as well as the denomination. Embedded into the paper, as well, it's visible only when held up to the light and can be read only with a magnifier.

The One for Five Scam

And speaking of that security strip, Leslie Kim, publisher of the *John Cooke Insurance Fraud Report*, demonstrated over dinner one night just how it can be torn out of a $5 bill and glued onto the back of a $1 bill so that when the bill is run through a changing machine, the machine will read the security code of the $5 bill and make change for that. I would like to add, this is *not* how we paid for our entrées.

Traveler's Checks

The same kinds of security features are used by the big manufacturers of traveler's checks—American Express, Bank of America, Thomas Cook and MasterCard—to thwart easily counterfeited bills. Each of them employs some or all of the following.

- Intaglio printing. In this process, a reverse image is etched onto a steel plate that is then pressed against the paper using twenty tons of pressure. This expensive process is the only way high-end printers and government printing offices can produce the kind of fine line detail that gives the "feel of money."

- Holograms produce that phenomenon whereby the image appears to move. Created by taking a three-dimensional photograph with a laser, it's used only on higher denomination traveler's checks. With phonies, it's rarely used at all.

- Microprinting can't be seen with the naked eye, nor can it be reproduced with a desktop scanner or color copier.

- MICR (magnetic ink character recognition) printing is the clumsy block lettering you see at the bottom of checks and traveler's checks. It can be legally reproduced with current desktop computer technology, using special software, quality laser printers and special magnetic ink toner cartridges.

- Ultraviolet ink is visible only when seen under a black light and is used on higher denomination bills. Water-based inks create the same effect but are revealed when slathered with water.

- Watermarks are an important anticounterfeiting device, as are special numbering codes embedded in the document.

Two Ways to Counterfeit

Because we have two kinds of perps here—the layman and the professional—there are also two different budgets, which will ultimately produce two different product qualities. Both methods have inherent flaws, recognizable by a trained clerk, and neither process can reproduce watermarks, ultraviolet inks or MICR printing.

- Offset printing manifests the better quality, varying, of course, with the printer's skill. This professional's method of choice can reproduce some of the microprinting, but the checks will appear flat and have no sheen since they are not manufactured by the intaglio printing method.

- Checks made on a color copier are the low-cost alternative and within almost anyone's skill level and budget. Alas, the knockoffs do not have the raised ink feel, fine line detail or microprinting of intaglio printing. Also, since the toner fuses the document, color-copied counterfeit checks have a flat, thick, shiny feel.

How Traveler's Checks Are Passed

Normally, traveler's checks are given out in a mall or on busy sidewalks over a long holiday weekend so the perps can be long gone before the string of frauds is discovered. Typically, a $100 check is used to pay for a $25 purchase, the thief pocketing the change.

Personal Check Fraud

The U.S. Justice Department estimates $10 billion worth of bad checks are passed each year. Declaring this the crime of the nineties, the Justice Department notes that since checks have no single standard, they're much easier to manufacture than, say, credit or ATM cards. All the forger need do is reproduce a check's basic ingredients—the remitter information, issuing bank, MICR lettering, account and check number—to have a passable facsimile.

In their latest bid to curb counterfeiting, the Federal Reserve Bank has instituted new standards such as padlock icons that instruct the reader to check the back where security features are further explained.

There are four types of bogus check drafts:

1. **Insufficient funds.** Here the perp simply writes a check for more money than is in the account. Hey, it happens. With the crook, it happens a lot. But with today's technology, such bogus checks are not so easily passed. Many retailers subscribe to a check guarantee company, or instruct their clerks to call a twenty-four-hour automated system to verify funds. Still, a perp can have $300 in his account, write twenty $299 checks on Friday night, and have them all verified as good.

2. **Stolen checks.** Individual checks are most often taken during a purse snatch or pickpocket attempt, along with the person's identification, and then passed just outside the victim's geographical area for easily resalable items such as TVs, VCRs and the like. Business checks are

even more attractive to thieves since a simple business card is considered valid identification by most outlets.

Thieves find both kinds of checks by "Dumpster-diving" for checks thrown away because the account has been closed. Wary clerks watch for suspects who don't bother to record the purchase, as well as those who try to distract them as they check ID.

3. **Wiped checks.** Here the perp takes an already processed check, erases the payee with an acid or organic solvent, and inserts his own name and often a new, higher amount, as well. The wiping process changes the paper's texture, which is a clue, as well as the fact that the checks are presented singularly, rather than all together in a checkbook. As of late, many check printers treat their new stock so the wiping process will not take.

4. **Homemade checks.** As with counterfeit currency and traveler's checks, color copiers and printers have turned many an amateur into a pro. And now that the software is available to manufacture one's own checks, there is nothing stopping the counterfeiter from simply printing checks on someone else's account. In fact, 20 percent of the $10 billion worth of bogus drafts passed each year are of the homegrown variety.

Forged Deposit Slips

This slick trick dates back to when mechanical readers were first introduced to the banking industry. Here, the crook simply places his own deposit slips on the bank's countertop so customers grab them instead of the blanks. Since nobody pays much attention to the blocky MICR numbers anyhow, and since the mechanical reader doesn't register the hand-written account number, every deposit made from that countertop goes directly into the crook's account.

This technique is still used by mom-and-pop teams, but since it's easily determined which account received the misdirected funds, it's a single-afternoon venture that must be abandoned by the end of the first day. Other than checking the automated system throughout the day, the only time investment is the fifteen minutes or so it takes to open the account.

Phony Charge Cards

For those trips down Rodeo Drive, it is necessary for the perp to have in his possession an actual facsimile of someone else's credit card. Not to worry, this can be accomplished in several ways.

Ordering a New Card

Perhaps the simplest method of obtaining another's credit card—other than outright theft—is to simply request a duplicate from the retailer. It is then sent either to the victim's "new" address (ironically, the same as the perp's) or to the victim's actual address and then intercepted or misdirected to a mail drop via a postal change-of-address card.

Forging Existing Cards

With a legitimate credit card, the embossed number on the front matches the magnetized strip coded on the back. To check for authenticity, the clerk is supposed to run the card through a swipe machine and then compare the embossed number with the machine's digital readout.

- Remagnetizing the strip. One way crooks manufacture phony credit cards is to steal someone else's (or buy a blank from a manufacturer) and then remagnetize the strip with a "cold" number, a legitimate credit card number not yet reported as stolen. Since the swipe machine doesn't read the embossed lettering, unless the clerk compares the card with the digital readout, the card will appear legitimate.

- Embossing and remagnetizing. Or the crook can buy or steal credit card blanks (legitimately sold to financial institutions, retailers and phone card companies) and then emboss a "cold" number, adding a magnetized strip to match. Now, if the clerk compares the two, they will match; *however*, the issuing bank printed across the top still will not coincide with the stolen card number. But to catch that, the clerk must actually look up the institution's code number in a security book—a rare occurrence, at best.

Bogus ATM Cards

Using a *shoulder-surfing* technique, the crook watches, either from close range or with the binoculars from the inside of a dark-windowed van, as the soon-to-be victim accesses his automatic teller machine. By noting his personal identification number (PIN) and matching it with the discarded receipt, the thief establishes the account number and PIN. Encoding a blank card with that data, crooks are then able to access the account. To counteract this practice, many banks have now installed little rearview mirrors at their ATMs and list just partial account numbers on receipts.

Check Kiting

Simply put, check kiting means establishing one checking account with a small balance and then writing a large check out of it to open another at a different financial institution. To cover the insufficient balance in the first, the confellow then writes a draft out of the second. Thus continues this round-robin, the confellow upping the ante a bit each time so he'll have a little extra cash for his trouble. Ambitious kiters get a whole slew of accounts going, the checks flying between them like a juggler tossing dishes at a street fair. So if nothing ever bounces, what's the big deal? There's no money, that's what, just a transference of paper that will eventually prove worthless once the chain is broken. But check kiting is not as easy as it once was. Now, not only are computers programmed to spot kiting patterns, most banks won't credit the full deposit until a check clears.

It should also be noted that many people "kite" their credit card balances from one card to another, which is not illegal unless it is done to gain as many material goods as possible as a prelude to going bankrupt.

Phone Fraud

With the examples above, some sort of currency or credit card is counterfeited in order to provide the perp with spending money. So what will they squander all this ill-gotten gain on? Certainly not calling their friends. What is the need of that when they can simply counterfeit a calling card, as well? The Communications Fraud Control Association puts phone fraud at a full 1 percent of long-distance carriers' $50 billion in annual revenues.

Calling Card Fraud

Perhaps the simplest way to phone free is to merely punch in somebody else's calling card number. This is, of course, a form of identity theft, but without the bother of collecting all that identifying data. Here all that's necessary is to steal the right combination of punchable numbers. This is normally done in one of two ways.

1. **Shoulder surfing.** The scoundrel loiters beside a phone booth, observing callers reaching out to touch someone. Since such dawdling can be a mite suspicious, true professionals accomplish this from a parked van with a pair of binoculars, much the way they shoulder-surf ATM passwords.

2. **Reprogramming the magnetic strip.** Another crook favorite is to reprogram prepaid phone cards so they will authorize unlimited dialing. This has become such a problem in Japan that the Nippon Telegraph and Telephone Corporation has changed many of its public telephones so they simply won't take phone card calls.

The Black Box

This illegal device emits a tone, allowing the caller to freely access long-distance lines.

Cellular Phone Cloning

Operating near a busy highway, high-tech crooks use sophisticated radio equipment to pick up a cell phone's ESN, or electronic serial number, which is a combination of the number dialed and the billing information, that is, the number of the cell phone.

That number is then reprogrammed into someone else's stolen cell phone (quite possibly mine) using illegally developed software. The end product—a cell phone stolen from one person coupled with a number taken from another—has a street price of about $150 and a life expectancy of just a couple of weeks, at which time the victim's bill comes in and he quite wisely changes his number. This is such a new crime that the policing agency, the Secret Service, simply has no statistics as yet.

Digital phones are said to be nonclonable, and now companies like CellularOne are offering their customers the option of turning off the phone's roaming feature while they're in town, rendering it less susceptible to thieves.

Merchandise

A counterfeit product is defined as an unauthorized copy of a product's name, logo or packaging. Virtually anything with brand-name recognition can be counterfeited. And it is—to the tune of $200 billion annually, a whole lot of jobs and, most heartbreaking of all, countless revenue lost to our beloved IRS.

The FBI's Organized Crime/Drug Operations Division names the counterfeiting of consumer products and the theft of intellectual rights as "the crime of the twenty-first century." Although admittedly just in this chapter alone we've had lots of claimants to that title, the fact is this underground industry is directly tied to organized crime, mainly because it offers two things criminals covet most: big profits and very little risk.

The Players

Any company with brand-name recognition can be knocked off, but the big losers are Rolex, Disney, Microsoft, Nike, and handbag manufacturers Louis Vuitton, Dooney & Bourke, and Coach.

The perps are usually ethnic gangs who feel safe operating outside the country, and rightly so, since their members are rarely prosecuted. Here are just a few who figured wrong.

- The Vietnamese gang Born To Kill (BTK) earned over $13 million with their counterfeit watch endeavor, as well as importing illegal immigrants and soliciting prostitution on the side. One perp is serving three consecutive life sentences for murder in connection with these activities.

- A Los Angeles Chinese gang was recently busted for manufacturing millions of dollars' worth of bogus Microsoft software. As a bonus, investigators netted a cache of military explosives and weapons. Another Chinese gang, the Triads, used the counterfeiting of software, pharmaceuticals, credit cards, apparel and accessories to launder drug money.

- The Islamic extremists linked to the World Trade Center bombing reportedly raised the cash for the venture by selling counterfeit products.

- The Irish Republican Army is known to fund their terrorist activities through the sale of counterfeit products.

As for the heat, the Guidry Group is one of the most prominent investigative groups around. They act as a liaison between manufacturers and the entities who prosecute trademark violations—the FBI, U.S. Customs, and state and local police, depending on jurisdiction. Mike McKenna, an investigative consultant with that firm, who provided much of the information for this chapter, says most cases are solved through informants' tips, undercover work, surveillance, and conducting pretense sales.

The Products

Many people downplay the ramifications of counterfeit merchandise by rationalizing the consumer is simply getting the same quality merchandise at a lower price. But there can be disastrous consequences to purchasing products not subject to U.S. quality controls. Dyes and inks might cause apparel to be highly flammable, shoddily manufactured toys might more easily be broken and swallowed, jewelry or pottery might contain dangerous amounts of lead, and food products might not meet FDA standards. It is up to the manufacturer to insure the safety of these products, and since counterfeiters generally don't follow federal guidelines, if they will cheat the company they ripped off, would they not cheat the consumer, as well?

By the way, the difference between a rip-off and a knockoff is whether the brand name is copied, as well.

Apparel

Again, any brand name is susceptible to rip-off, and the more expensive the product, the greater the return on the counterfeiter's investment. One skiwear firm estimates their annual loss at $1 million; an eyewear company puts theirs at several times that per month. Biggest manufacturing rip-off areas: Italy, the Pacific Rim and Korea.

- Watches. Counterfeiters import "blanks," which is legal, and then have the trademark stamped here in the United States. Do customers know they're getting a fake? Most do, says McKenna. If a Rolex is purchased at a flea market for $20, then certainly so. But if the watches are distributed to a retail outlet, they will command the Rolex prices, and that is passed along to the consumer.

- Handbags. Louis Vuitton, Dooney & Bourke, and Coach are some of the most coveted brands by counterfeiters. Again, the blanks are manufactured overseas and snuck into the United States.

- Sunglasses. Counterfeit copies have been known to shatter easily and fail to protect from ultraviolet rays as advertised.

- Designer and sports apparel. The high-end products take the biggest hits; Nike takes the lead.

Automobile and Aviation Parts

Aviation officials believe a counterfeit clutch was responsible for a 1987 helicopter crash that killed a traffic reporter during a live broadcast. Upon investigation, detectives found more than six hundred helicopters sold to NATO and civilians alike were equipped with counterfeit parts, putting their occupants at risk. In 1989, a Norwegian plane crash killed fifty-five people, and authorities said U.S. counterfeiters were to blame. And in 1991, the *San Francisco Chronicle* reported counterfeit brake pads were the culprit in a collision that killed a mother and child. All told, U.S. automobile manufacturers and suppliers are said to be losing $12 billion annually, as well as 210,000 jobs, to the counterfeit industry. Biggest counterfeit manufacturing areas: Mexico and Russia.

Baby Formula

In 1995, authorities discovered a counterfeit version of a popular brand of infant formula in Safeway and other stores in at least sixteen states. The FDA issued an alert, warning consumers to watch out for the fictitious bar code and expiration date.

Computer Software and Electronics

Experts estimate more than 40 percent of all U.S. software revenues go to bogus manufacturers. In other countries, as many as 90 percent of all copies sold are counterfeit. Biggest manufacturing area: the Pacific Rim.

Pharmaceutical and Medical Devices

The illegal manufacturing of drugs is especially disconcerting to people who are desirous of knowing what they're putting into their bodies. Biggest manufacturing areas: Mexico, South America and Spain.

Consider these true incidents:

- A counterfeit version of Tagamet was the cause of at least one woman's bleeding ulcer.

- Phony concoctions of the antibiotic Ceclor were blamed for a seven-state bout of painful ear infections and possible ear damage in children.

- Retin-A, manufactured in Mexico, originally seen as a steal at $2 instead of $20, proved a bust when the product was determined to be merely vitamin A cream colored with food dye.

- The FDA recalled $7 million worth of heart pumps already placed in patients, after they discovered counterfeit parts used to make them were malfunctioning.

- And, surprise! In 1981, over a million imitation birth control pills were distributed to unsuspecting women, resulting in unwanted pregnancies and irregular bleeding.

Toiletries and Cosmetics

Procter & Gamble's Head and Shoulders shampoo took the hit in August 1995 when the Ohio-based company felt compelled to place a half-page national advertisement warning consumers that counterfeit versions of their product could harm folks with weakened immune systems.

Toys

Because counterfeiters don't follow federal guidelines, children are more susceptible to choking on poorly manufactured products or being poisoned by toxic paints. Here it is the customer who can be the big loser. Biggest manufacturing area: the Pacific Rim.

Videotapes

The television show *Seinfeld* did a hilarious bit on Kramer's friend Brody, who got Jerry involved in illegally filming movies for bootlegging purposes, but most low-end pirated videotapes are the result of simply ignoring that scary FTC warning at the start of the show and illegally duplicating the movie for distribution. The pros, however, manage to obtain illegally taped copies of new movies and have them out on the street even before they're released to the theaters. Biggest manufacturing areas: Russia, Italy and neighborhood video shops.

How to Spot Counterfeit Merchandise

Counterfeit merchandise aimed directly at the consumer shows up everywhere from street vendors to swap meets to sports stadiums to retail stores. The International AntiCounterfeiting Coalition based in Washington, DC, says to look for:

- Inferior Packaging. The printing is blurred, the labels are mismatched or ripped, and/or there is shoddy stitching.
- Suspect Merchant Information. The location is wrong; the 800 number is missing; the codes, trademarks, copyrights, bar codes, recycling signs and holograms are incorrect.
- Product Data. Words are misspelled, brand names are

altered, or there are drastic changes in content, color, smell or packaging.

- The Price. Be wary of cut-rate prices.

Identity Cards

There are roughly four kinds of customers buying phony IDs in today's marketplace: the underage youth, the illegal immigrant, the credit-impaired person and the out-and-out criminal. Doing it is simple, of course. Just trot on down to the far side of town and ask around on the street corner. Via computers and color printers, making up a reasonable facsimile of an ID from some other state is child's play.

Nigerian Style

Amazingly, Nigerians are able to obtain as many official government identity cards as they have a mind to. Leslie Kim, publisher of the *John Cooke Insurance Fraud Report*, says since there hasn't been, until recently, any kind of centralized population recording machine in that country, folks get born, married and die without the kind of vital statistics documentation essential to our system. When they need identification papers of some sort (like for travel to the U.S.), this credential is easily obtained simply by filling out an affidavit swearing they are who they say they are and, by their own signature, self-notarizing the document. That statement is then witnessed by someone who knows them. And that, as they say, is that.

Since the entire system is built on trust, what do you suppose happens when an applicant is untrustworthy? Could it be that this person goes back again and again, creating totally fictitious people for which there is now official documentation on each? You betcha.

Now, when this same person heads for our shores, he has twenty or so identity cards, all of them valid official documents issued by the Nigerian government. Each identity then takes on a life of its own, obtaining student loans, credit, long-distance phone service, bank accounts, etc.—and then, in turn, defaulting on all of those.

Identity Theft

Experts agree that identity theft—the counterfeiting of a person's identifying data in order to use their credit to procure goods and services—is now America's fastest-growing crime. In fact, at the time of this writing, it is such a new phenomenon that there is not even one central organization to which these crimes are reported! Because of that, no statistics exist, but San Francisco PD's fraud inspector Earl Wismer says identity theft now accounts for almost 60 percent of his caseload. And why? Because methods put in place years ago to render our lives more convenient—credit cards, automatic teller machines, phone calling cards—require, by their very nature, a limited verification of the user's identity in order to work.

A perp with a case of identity theft might not be awfully visible but it could certainly account for why a "jobless" suspect can live like a king. And because writers often have a need to misdirect the reader's attention, this chapter might be worth noting.

An Overview

Local fraud inspectors, the FBI, CIA and other top cops find these new cases a challenge to the methods they've traditionally used to fight crime. Because there are almost always multiple jurisdictions involved, the logistics are often insurmountable. Additionally, they have developed no way of identifying the anonymous caller, and even when the merchandise is accepted by the thief, there is no way to prove he was the one who ordered it. And, of course, as with all cons, DAs are often so inundated with violent crimes they're forced to ignore such "harmless" offenses as screwing up the rest of someone else's life.

Identity theft is accomplished in one of two ways.

1. **Account takeover scams.** The perp taps into existing bank and credit accounts, orders duplicate credit cards or additional goods and services, and continues until the fraud is discovered when the bill comes in. In a variation on this theme, a postal change-of-address card is used

to misdirect the victim's mail, further delaying discovery of the theft.

2. **True party frauds.** The perp establishes new accounts using the victim's identifying information. Now the prey has no clue as to the fraud until the creditors start hounding him months later. In either case, authorities argue the victim is not a victim since there is no monetary loss. (After a fight, it is the merchant who "eats" the charges.) Still, the ensuing credit problems can last a lifetime, thwarting the victim's future dreams, such as the purchasing of a home.

What It Looks Like

One day a self-employed interior decorator called with a problem. Six months before, she'd gotten a holler from a major department store saying she'd made no payments on a credit card she didn't even know she had. The balance: over $11,000.

Unfortunately, this was just the tip of the iceberg. From there, the phone rang almost daily with calls from businesses claiming she owed them for things she'd never bought. In all, the demands totalled over $82,000, including a $30,000 line of credit from her very own bank.

Finally, one sympathetic bill collector was able to provide her with an address where the goods had been shipped— to her same name in a town thirty miles north of the small coastal community in which she lived. The woman finally reached a police detective who'd, ironically, had his identity stolen, as well, and so took an interest and was able to arrest the thief. Amazingly, despite the perp's detailed confession— she'd obtained identifying data by hiring a private eye to run the victim's credit report—she was released on bail, moved to another community and continued to receive goods and services charged to this same victim.

Meanwhile, my client was hounded by collection agencies galore, and neither the DA, FBI or CIA would take on her case. They all labeled her a victim by chance, confirming there was nothing she could have done to prevent what happened to her, yet since she was out no actual money, they claimed there was no loss.

That, in a nutshell, is identity theft.

The Players

Authorities agree the only 100 percent safe way for consumers to protect themselves against having their identity stolen is not to have one. Credit reporting agencies have tried to argue that the victim isn't one because it's the retailers who are eating the charges. While that's true, in August of 1996, a Los Angeles jury awarded an identity theft victim $200,000, because they ruled TransUnion failed to correct her credit reports in a timely fashion.

As for the perps, basically they can be divided into two categories: the person who knows the victim, and the person who doesn't. When you think how little it takes to impersonate someone—"We must verify it's you. What are the last four digits of your Social Security number?"—it's no wonder so many perps turn out to be family, acquaintances, co-workers or legitimate employees of the very institutions who issued the victims credit in the first place.

Fraud Guy

Our office has a steady caller who's tried every trick in the book to become a client, even though the service we provide him is continually slow, overpriced and, in the end, frustratingly nonexistent.

Fraud Guy has been calling for almost a year now, at the rate of about once a month. The first time, he stated he already had the name and address of the person he was interested in, he just needed a "Social" and "DOB." After dropping this insiders' lingo, he said he'd wait on hold while we ran the information. He didn't even bother to ask the price.

Well aware that the Social Security number and date of birth are the exact data necessary to perpetrate identity theft, my chief investigator, Ann Flaherty, put him on hold as we discussed the situation. As she often does when it comes to sticky public relations problems, she turned the matter over to me. I picked up, with a cheery, "Can I help you?" and he again requested the information.

I asked him why he needed it, and he said he was a skip tracer, another insider term. *Hmmm.* A skip tracer's job is to *find* people. Yes, they often need the SSN and DOB to do so; most times, however, they already have that information, per the credit application. But since Fraud Guy already knew his subject's whereabouts, there was simply no further use for such information. Except, of course, to perpetrate identity theft. And Fraud Guy couldn't very well pretend he needed to find the person, since the full name and address was the only way he had of relaying to us exactly who he wanted to find. He'd worked himself into a bit of a corner, you might say.

But logic didn't faze Fraud Guy. When the skip-tracer story got him put on hold while we ate our lunches, he switched to the standing-in-the-courthouse-with-his-attorney tale. When our computers went down on that one, he segued into the on-the-road-on-business yarn.

Another tip-off was Fraud Guy's straight-to-business MO. With a regular customer, you simply cannot get them off the phone. They are invariably obsessed with determining the location of their subject, having no idea of the usefulness of identifying data such as SSN and DOB in order to accomplish that task. As a detective, you have to wade through how they met their honey sixty-seven years ago at the corner of Fifth and Mission, and every conversation they've had with her since, including how full the moon was on the night they parted. And you're often asked if a photo would be helpful, as if they expect you to hang out on the street corner, peering into the faces of passersby.

But Fraud Guy never bothered with such touching tales. Clearly, he didn't want to spend a lot of time honing some phony story, he just wanted the data he needed to screw another victim. In the end, no matter what succinct scenario he came up with, these components always gave him away.

- He was always seeking identifying data, never the location of the subject. Since there are only two reasons for anyone to want identifying data—in order to locate someone, or in order to impersonate someone—his motive was clear.

- He always offered a credit card as payment. No price was ever discussed, since he had no intention of compensating us for our services.

- He'd insist on waiting while we ran the reports. By playing on this sense of urgency, Fraud Guy undoubtedly hoped we'd provide the information before charging the card. When we didn't fall for that, he'd call back in a few minutes. He'd never provide us with a call-back number, claiming he wasn't anywhere he could be reached.

- He never offered any explanation as to why he required the information. When questioned, he made his story as short as possible.

Now while Fraud Guy was on hold, Ann and I would invariably do the same things. We would complain about our social lives. File our nails. Wipe the meter maid's two-hour chalk mark off our tires. Between these activities, we'd also check to see if the credit card he'd offered as payment had been reported as compromised, phone the card company with a possible "Code 10" (possible stolen credit card) and attempt to notify both victims—the one whose card he'd already acquired, and the one on whom he was seeking identifying data.

It took only about nine months for Fraud Guy to figure out this wasn't going to work. But try as we might, we were unable to nab him, because he was always just a voice on a pay phone, giving up none of himself in the process.

Then Fraud Guy perfected his MO—and got me. Ann was out of the office when Fraud Guy called with the debut of the standing-in-the-courthouse story, which he hadn't used up until then. It sounded like him, but when he provided— for the first time—a call-back number, I put my qualms aside and ran the data, charged the card and called him back with the information.

The next time he phoned with a similar scenario, Ann was a lot more astute and put him on hold while she gave him the usual runaround. Now I had to fess up to Ann that I'd been had. We agreed, call-back number or not, we'd give Fraud Guy no more information. Our stints as good public citizens extended to alerting the victims and the credit card company, but still we couldn't *catch* him.

Then he offered a new twist; he wanted to set up a prepaid account. He wanted to send a $300 cashier's check and replace it when it ran out. Now, I don't know how much you know about the detective business, but this *never* happens. Never. Ever.

With a roll of her eyes, Ann handed me the phone, and I proceeded to quiz this self-proclaimed "skip tracer" for all the information we required in order to set up an account: name, address, SSN, DOB, credit card number, references and, of course, why he needed the data. "What!" he exploded. "I'll be paying in advance with a cashier's check. Why do you need all that?"

"Because, *Fraud Guy,*" I said, clearly having had it with him. "The kind of information you are requesting is the exact data necessary to perpetrate identity theft. Now this wouldn't be much of a company if we just blithely gave such data out to any slimebag that happened to call. Now would we?"

Identity theft, he pondered. Why, he'd heard of that. Seen it on some TV show. He declined to give me further information, instead musing that perhaps it was time he subscribed to one of these databases himself. Could I recommend one?

Oh, yeah, right.

That was the last time Fraud Guy called, but there was one last sad event. The one instance I got caught, I became a victim, as well. The $25 credit card charge was protested by the true cardholder, and I had to eat the search.

So the score remains: Fraud Guy, one; Rat Dog, zero.

Procuring the Information

It used to be that the number one way to snare another's good name was the dead-baby method: Find a child who died before being issued their first MasterCard, order their birth certificate and build an identity from ground up. Today, because goods and services can be ordered via phone or fax, there's no longer a need for procuring such documents. Rifling a restaurant's trash can yield hoards of credit card receipts, each bearing all the data necessary to commit identity theft. Or if the perp prefers day work, tossing a suburban mailbox will generate pretty much the same haul, as will hacking into the Internet. Card numbers can also be obtained by any number of scams, including tricking the data out of an unsuspecting private investigator. Gulp.

Does it take a brilliant hacker to break into the Internet and steal identifying data? Not according to Peter Shipley, a Berkeley, California, consultant who makes his living by trying to break into the computers of private companies (at their request). "Most sites are basically exploitable through one method or another," he says. Citing only one exception, he says every site he tested was a piece of cake.

That also is what Carlos Felipe Salgado Jr. thought. The self-employed computer technician, was labeled a *kode kiddie* by Yobie Benjamin, chief knowledge officer at Cambridge Technology Partners in Cambridge, Massachusetts. This is insider lingo for someone who employs known hacking methods rather than formulating their own. "It's akin to stealing a key to someone's home rather than picking the lock," says Benjamin.

Unfortunately, after Salgado went to all the trouble of collecting a hundred thousand credit card numbers, he made his one and only sale to an FBI agent. On the day his trial was to begin, he pleaded guilty in federal court to unauthorized access to a computer, trafficking in stolen credit card numbers, and possessing more than fifteen stolen credit card numbers with intent to defraud. At the time of this writing, Salgado faces up to 30 years in prison and a $1 million fine.

BILKING BUSINESSES

"Dear Insurance Company,
By the time you read this letter, I will have been
accidently run over and killed by the 3:45 P.M. downtown
bus."

—The John Cooke
Insurance Fraud
Report

Just as confellows target individuals, so they also work their magic on modest to immensely sized business enterprises. Some undoubtedly rationalize that a company cannot be considered a victim since it has no feelings. Others justify their actions by claiming businesses budget to absorb a certain amount of loss, and therefore screwing them to the wall is the natural order of things. Others don't bother with any excuses at all because they're too busy thinking about what they can buy with all that money.

In his most excellent memoir, *Catch Me If You Can,* Frank W. Abagnale Jr. takes great pride in the fact that he swindled only big businesses—except for the time he tricked an arrogant hooker into paying *him* for her services. Indeed, as much as I loathe the concept, I thoroughly enjoyed the book and came away thinking what a Robin-Hoody kind of guy Frank was. If you want to write about a lovable confellow, it might be best to stay away from the kind who takes shaky moms to the bank and consider the memoirs of someone like Frank, who steals from the rich and gives to hungry blonde flight attendants alone on a layover in Paris.

Telephone Fraud

Basically, you've got your standard boiler-room operation as outlined in the chapter "Let the Buyer Beware," but here the victims are not chosen for their greed or gullibility, but simply because they exist.

Bust Out Schemes

Capitalizing on common business practices whereby wholesalers and suppliers traditionally accommodate new customers with credit, these confellows create phony references and then make token payments while they're selling off their ill-gotten bounty at bargain-basement prices. By the time the supplier has figured out he's not getting paid, the con man has either disappeared or declared bankruptcy.

Office Equipment Scam

The teleshark phones a small business, asking to speak to whoever purchases the office equipment. After the business manager explains they require nothing, thank you very much, the confellow asks about existing equipment—makes, model numbers and the like. The manager politely chitchats and hangs up, never suspecting a thing.

What's really happening? The teleshark uses the gathered intelligence to send out unsolicited supplies—copier toner, computer paper, ink cartridges, etc.—along with an invoice. Usually the company will simply unpack the supplies and route the bill to accounting, who will dutifully pay it. Without a little comparison thinking, nobody figures out the products were not only never ordered, they were overpriced and of inferior quality, as well.

PBX Line Theft

The latest twist in phone fraud is the victimizing of businesses by tapping into their private branch exchange

(PBX) that allows employees to dial into the home office via an 800 or WATS line.

The system works by letting the employee utilize a feature called *reorigination* to bypass calling card charges by punching in a personal ID number. To swipe one of these three- to four-digit security codes, computer hackers program their personal computers to sequentially dial numbers until they hit on the right combination. It's not as tedious as you might think, since the hacker can actually start the program before he goes nighty-night and have the security code cracked by the time he wakes up in the morning.

To combat fraudulently accessed PBX numbers, Sprint has designed a device that recognizes the user's voice pattern. The caller simply speaks his identification number, and the system verifies his legitimate use of the system.

Door-To-Door Duplicity

With the exception of a very few companies, almost the only legitimate door-to-door sales going on in America today are directed at businesses, simply because these are the only sales calls where the potential customers all require the same things, for example, bottled water, postage meters and office supplies. Unlike residential salesguys, most of these hard workers are on the level. But, alas, not all.

Con Cruise

The four-color brochure offered "Champagne Cruises" for a "Special Limited-Time Offer." For $39.95, six people would get "Complimentary Appetizers, Dancing, On-Board Entertainment, and Fun in the Sun"—a $210 package. The fine print mentioned something about a $3 boarding pass and a two-beverage minimum, and there was a little MasterCard and Visa symbol snuggling in the corner.

One company owner wrote the "Ask Rat Dog" column, complaining that it took her seven months to book the excursion. Every time she called she was informed, via a recording, that that month's dates were sold out and to try again on a certain day, several weeks hence. If she missed that deadline by even a day, she had to wait another month to call. When the woman finally arrived with her employees, the cashier stated the additional $72 was payable only in cash, regardless of what the brochure stated. Embarrassed, she had to borrow $20 from one of her subordinates in order to come aboard.

From there, they were herded onto an overcrowded vessel, with chairs for less than a third of the occupants. The "appetizers" were one bowl of cold pasta salad and another of chickenless chicken salad. The drink coupons could be exchanged for champagne—or diet Coke. (I guess "diet Coke Cruise" didn't have the same ring.) As for the "On-Board Entertainment," the piped-in music could be heard beneath the din of people fighting over the cold pasta salad.

In one of our most renowned stings ever, Ask Rat Dog budgeted enough to investigate this seafaring operation first-hand. Disguised as five Beautiful but Curious Party Girls, we broke up into groups of one and immediately discovered there was no representative from the promotional company on board. Our second finding was that while the drink coupons purchased prior to boarding cost $4.50, purchasing a drink on-board cost $.50 less.

In determining whether an ad is considered false advertising, it is important to isolate the promises and determine the level of fulfillment. Here are our findings:

1. *Complimentary Appetizers* was technically correct since there *were* two items.

2. *On-Board Entertainment* was technically correct since there was taped background music—which is, admittedly, a little like proclaiming an elevator has On-Lift Entertainment.

3. *Fun in the Sun* was technically correct since the sun came out that day, the boat had outside access, and I run with a fun crowd.

4. *Dancing* was technically correct as long as one didn't require a band, disc jockey or dance floor in order for people to fling themselves around the room.

5. *Limited-Time Offer.* Here, the company clearly stepped

over the line. When the expiration date on the brochure lapsed, it was routinely replaced with an identical offer.

6. *Major Credit Cards Accepted.* Sorry, fellahs. Simply not so.

A more truthful brochure might have read: "Two Completely Taste-free Dishes! Taped Music Barely Audible! Feel Free to Frolic at Will!" Although they received a bargain cruise instead of the impressive one in the brochure, any pigeons who were finally able to book would merely grumble, but no one in their right mind would sue. Very few would think to gripe to the DA's consumer complaint division.

Another perfect blow-off for a quasi-legal scam.

Internet Specialties

How many times am I doomed to quote *Globe Magazine*'s wise counsel, "Wherever there is an opportunity, there's an opportunist"? Internet scams did not exist fifteen years ago, chiefly because neither did the World Wide Web. Unfortunately, this medium has gotten a reputation for being "sophisticated" and "intellectual," when the truth is con artists play on these presumptions to weave their own brand of reality.

E-mail Blackmail

Via electronic mail, the business receives a downloaded copy of their own Web site ad, an invoice and a letter declaring the Web page arrived in a certain unsolicited E-mail box, in violation of federal law restricting such happenings. The confused company is told to pay up or face being sued for breaching Section 227(b)(3)(B) of U.S. Code Title 47. Quaking at phrases like, "you have been legally warned," more than one firm has fallen for this one.

What's really happening? It's a scam! The confellow has simply cruised the Internet, downloaded random Web sites and forged his own E-mail address at the top to make it look legit. Unbelievably, one such scammer tried this on the Consumer Fraud Alert Network, which is akin to attempting to scam the Better Business Bureau. In a follow-up phone call, the cocky con then claimed he was in his car on the way to the courthouse and they'd better pay up posthaste or face the consequences. He added, and I quote, "This is no joke. The more questions you ask, the more trouble you are getting into."

Ohhhhh, you're scaring me, Con Guy! Not counting on the Network's chummy contacts within the esteemed halls of the IRS and FTC, this fellow might just have bitten off more than he can possibly choke on.

Direct-Mail Malfeasance

Again, as with the "Let the Buyer Beware" chapter, almost every direct-mail piece targeting businesses where there is a single-item offering is a scam. Here are but a few.

Solicitations Disguised as Invoices

Remember the office equipment scam, where the con guy sends along supplies that were never ordered? Well, in this variation on a theme, no product is ever sent—just the invoice! To stay just this side of the law (Title 39 of the U.S. Code, Section 3001, to be exact, which prohibits the mailing of a solicitation in the form of an invoice), the conner will state the notice is a "solicitation." Just not in very big letters.

Yellow Page Invoice

It looks like *the* yellow pages—even has the snappy walking fingers so admired by millions. And so the pigeon pays for what he thinks is his yearly advertisement in the phone book.

What's really happening? It's not an invoice, but yet another solicitation from an alternative publisher capitalizing on the fact that the walking fingers logo and name "Yellow Pages" are not protected by federal trademark nor copyright registration. Again, to stay just this side of the law, itsy bitsy letters proclaim it is a solicitation, not an invoice, but the perception is that of the phone company, so it is often paid.

Government Warning

An official-looking form arrives announcing a law that appears is not being complied with. In our case, it is the one stating something about employee withholdings and benefits.

What's really happening? It's not the U.S. government, but a small independent one working out of a post office box. Preying on the fears of busy yet uninformed business owners, they solicit money for services that can be gotten for free from agencies like the IRS or Social Security.

Insurance Fraud

By far the largest private enterprise targeted by con artists is the insurance biz. Anytime anything is insurable—a car, personal property, home, business, health, jewelry, even a pet—the promise of a guaranteed payoff will lure a certain number of con artists anxious to collect on that promise.

Now sometimes insurance fraud is simply a crime of opportunity—making the most (financially) of a bad situation—but professional perps consider clumsiness and collision a lifelong pursuit. Whichever, the policing of this billion-dollar racket is tackled by the fraud division of each state's department of insurance, which works hand in hand with the insurance companies, as well as the National Insurance Crime Bureau (NICB), which acts as a liaison between the two and helps investigate suspicious claims.

Workers' Compensation Fraud

Not *workman's* comp, as J.J. Jacobson, California Department of Insurance, Fraud Division, reminds me, since it is politically uncool to insinuate only men perpetrate this crime. Bottom line, no matter what the sex, what you've got here is an employee faking or exaggerating an injury in order to collect from their boss's insurance company. Here are the three main areas of fraud J.J.'s office deals with.

Applicant Fraud

The employee makes the claim. There are three ways to perpetrate fraud.

1. There is no injury. The worker is simply lying. There might have been an accident, but there is no injury.
2. There's a lesser injury. There was an accident, and there

is some physical damage, but it's been exaggerated by the claimant.

3. The injury is not job related. There was an injury, but it happened while waterskiing, not window cleaning.

Commercial or Professional Fraud.

Here, someone acts on behalf of the employee, traditionally an attorney or health care provider. Whether it means making the boo-boo bigger than is warranted, securing payment for services not rendered, overbilling or treating the uninjured, when caught, health care providers have very little defense, since they are trained to recognize an injury when they see one.

Workers' Compensation Fraud Mill

This is an organized group of applicants, lawyers and health care providers who regularly and systematically defraud insurance companies. Always on the lookout for potential patient/clients, they employ the services of a *capper* who hangs around unemployment offices, looking for people on disability, and police stations, where people go to pick up accident reports. Some even have hospital snitches on retainer who routinely pocket the throwaway copies of medical reports and then contact the patients, inquiring if they are up to a little game of fraud.

When all three legs of this triangle exist—the attorney, health care provider and capper—investigators consider it a mill. The attorney may work with a half-dozen health care providers, who in turn liaison with other shysters, but detectives find the same names popping up again and again. In a mill, there's no legitimate high-tech equipment, just "props": an "orthion" table, massage chair and/or an X-ray machine stored in a closet, perhaps.

To prove it's a mill, investigators check whether:

- The doctor sees an unusually high number of patients.
- He prescribes the same treatment for everyone, regardless of injuries.

- The billing is in line with the injury, as described in the medical report.

Deciding if they can prosecute is determined by the answers to these four questions:

- Did the applicant get injured due to employment?
- Are there any witnesses?
- Did the applicant file a fraudulent claim?
- Can we prove it?

Auto Insurance Fraud

The second kind of con involves one of Americans' favorite insurable assets, the automobile. Since vehicles are routinely covered for theft, collision and personal injury, these obviously are the areas scam artists target for their claims. Auto fraud basically falls into two categories.

Stolen Vehicles and Property

For most people, it is a traumatic experience to have their car stolen. But crooks not only invite theft, they invite it back. There are two ways insurance fraud is committed when claiming a vehicle or property was stolen: staged thefts and inflated claims on legitimate incidents.

There are three ways staged thefts are accomplished:

1. **Vehicle destroyed or abandoned.** Perp No. 1 gives her keys to Perp No. 2, instructing him to steal her car while she's enjoying pot roast at Grandma's. Perp No. 2 drives it fifty miles south, strips and abandons the vehicle, or drives it over a cliff. Perp No. 1 collects the insurance, often inflating the value of the contents inside, and divvies up the proceeds between them.

2. **Vehicle sold for scrap.** Perp No. 2 takes the car to a chop shop, where they disassemble it and sell the parts, or alter the "vin" (vehicle identification number) and hawk the whole dang thing.

3. **Vehicle stored or shipped to another country.** The car is never stolen at all. Gypsies are but one of the groups who have been known to hide the vehicle in a storage

facility and retrieve it many years later. Others have gone so far as to ship the car off to another country via cargo container.

Automobile Accidents

To spot fraudulent claims, investigators look for those claimants overeager for a speedy settlement. They are unusually willing to take the blame and exceptionally knowledgeable with insurance, medical or vehicle repair terminology.

- Two-car collision. The first way staged accidents are orchestrated is by two folks simply running into each other, usually in a parking lot where the cops are unlikely to be called. Each report the accident either as a hit-and-run, or a collision between vehicles.

- Swoop and squat. This is insider lingo for an incident where the inciting vehicle swoops in and goes squat to cause the accident, and the second vehicle is an unwilling participant. Typically, the perps drive older, less expensive cars and target late-model, more costly, and therefore well-insured, vehicles.

    In one of the most dramatic swoop-and-squat cases to date, on June 17, 1992, a swoop car, complete with four passengers, cut in front of a big rig, figuring the company would have deep pockets. In this instance, instead of the $1,000 worth of damage the perps aimed at, the truck jackknifed, fell onto them and crushed one passenger to death. In that moment, insurance fraud turned into manslaughter.

    In another 1997 incident, a swoop car cut in front of a supermarket's big rig that was traveling in front of a passenger car with a family of three inside. Still, everything would have been "fine" except the cement truck behind the passenger car couldn't stop, plowed into it and pushed it under the big rig, causing it to explode, incinerating all inside.

Common elements frequently present in phony claims are:

- The vehicle is rented.
- There are three or four passengers on board.

- No police report is taken.
- The accident happens shortly after the vehicle is insured, just before the policy is due to expire, or as soon as the coverage is upped.
- The claimant gives a post office box or hotel as his address.
- The claimant has been one before.
- The claimant changes his phone number and/or address several times per claim.

Staged Accident Mills

In the September/October 1997 issue of the *John Cooke Insurance Fraud Report*, G. Andrew Nagle stated, "It is not an unusual circumstance for a driver to go out into traffic and become involved in multiple accidents in a single day. He may come back to the 'home base' only long enough to pick up an alternate vehicle or load up a new set of passengers. Then it's back to the freeway to seek the next victim."

Obviously, there's big money in this. In April of 1996, Sherman Oaks, California attorney Noel Stephen Olshan was arrested for organizing a staged accident mill, authorities placing the take at $20 million in about seven years of operation. Staged accidents are accomplished in one of three ways:

1. **Paper accidents.** These mishaps don't actually happen. The damage has occurred prior and under different circumstances. If the adjustor is trained, he'll notice the points of impact don't match the story.

2. **Trickery accidents.** In this Gypsy exclusive, the perps watch as an elderly woman drives into a parking lot. As she shops, they then draw a black mark alongside her vehicle, and then accuse her of hitting them as she starts to drive away. The intimidating group demands compensation, often by threatening she'll lose her license if she reports back to her insurance company. They may even follow her home for additional funds and/or to finger her for further cons.

3. **Legitimate accidents.** These can also be fraudulent if the vehicle or medical damage report is inflated.

Signs of a Fraudulent Claim

Since there are two kinds of claims made in auto accidents, there are also two kinds of fraudulent claims.

With a vehicle damage claim, there are four major signs that damage is nonexistent or overinflated.

1. All the vehicles are taken to the same repair shop.
2. The collision is minor but the estimate isn't.
3. There's no accompanying towing charge for the supposedly undrivable car.
4. The body shop or claimant discourages the appraiser from visiting the vehicle.

And with claimants fraudulently reporting medical damage, there are four signs, as well.

1. There are unrelated occupants in the vehicle, all of whom contact the same lawyer or doctor.
2. The collision is minor, yet all injuries are of the "subjectively diagnosed" variety—headaches, whiplash, muscle spasms, etc. Also, the medical bills are much higher than the minor accident would warrant.
3. The invoices are photocopies, often third or fourth generation, and do not itemize visits or therapy. They show the patient receiving routine treatment on weekends and holidays.
4. The attorney's letter is dated the same day as the accident.

Life Insurance

Since the mystery genre requires the positioning of a body sometime in the first chapter, and since rigor mortis normally occurs as the result of an accident, suicide, murder or illness, writers are always looking for new ways to get their victims into this stiff state. But because this is a book on con games, nothing is, of course, ever as it seems. And so with that murder on page one, it just might prove to be that the victim is not, sob, dead after all!

Such was the case of the Filipino dentist who immigrated to the United States and then proceeded to terrorize his wife to such a degree that she fled for her life, taking their six-year-old son with her. The doc, who'd already had her insured twice over, figured she was gone for good so why not cash in on the $110,000 in insurance he'd already purchased? As proof of her demise, he presented a Filipino death certificate and Malaysian police report. Red flag! Whenever folks take an overseas dirt nap, insurance companies smell rats galore, says one fraud inspector who prefers to remain nameless, primarily due to my mixing of metaphors. In any case, in this instance the insurance carrier hired an Asian-based private eye who discovered the documents were bogus.

Yet, no "case closed" on this one. First, by law the claim had to be forwarded to the Department of Insurance (DOI) for a look-see. It then ran a DMV check on the long-gone mom, only to discover she'd applied for a new driver's license seven months after her untimely demise.

Ohhhhh, this does not look good for the dentist. But before the DOI could take him down, it had to be established that the doc was the author of those phony documents, and that they weren't just the result of some unbelievable bureaucratic snafu. And since evidence collected oversees by foreign detectives is inadmissible, the DOI needed to verify the documents themselves, as well as catch him in a confession, or at least a contradiction.

Using the excuse that the DOI is responsible for making sure insurance companies are providing quality service, they called the doc in and asked if he'd personally obtained the recording documents. Of course, he acknowledged, adding to the pile a certificate of cremation showing where his wife's ashes were scattered, as well as the names of several witnesses to her fatal crash. But the coup de grâce was when he offered that he'd personally viewed her body as it lay in the coffin.

Having already confirmed the police report was bogus and the death certificate a whited-out version of a male gunshot victim, the investigator showed the dentist a series of driver's license photos of his wife, which he identified, including the one taken seven months after he'd viewed her corpse. Upon being shown the date of that application, he fell apart and confessed, stamping his guilt like an embossed seal on the cover of the report. Because of Miranda requirements, the investigators were not yet prepared to make an arrest, and unfortunately, by the time they were, the dentist had fled back to Manila.

Red Flags

In the case above, it was the exotic demise that red-flagged the claim and propelled the investigation into action. So, just in case you are planning insurance fraud—on paper, of course—you should be aware of these other high signs that might cause your perp a bit of trouble.

- It's a brand-new policy. And by brand-new, the insurance industry means it was issued less than two years before the person's death.

- There's a sudden increase in coverage. No point in knocking off a mate for $10,000 when you can get $110,000 for the same accidental arrow through the forehead.

- The coverage is out of proportion to the person's net worth. Let's face it, some folks just aren't worth $10 million. Since the very purpose of insurance is to shield the beneficiary against financial hardship, it might make sense for a child to be insured for $5,000 or $6,000 to cover burial expenses, but not for $1 million. Most insurance companies just won't issue such policies, but if they do and there is a claim, the case has more red flags on it than a Russian county fair.

- The death certificate and other burial documents are photocopied.

- Multiple death certificates are ordered from Vital Statistics. Since insurance companies demand originals, checking to see how many copies the beneficiary has ordered can lead to additional policies on the same person.

Nice in Theory

This is not to say insurance adjusters actually pick up on such clues. Although many utilize the services of the National Insurance Crime Bureau (NICB) for investigative services, some either just don't get it, or just don't care. The carrier has two years to contest a suspect claim, and the courts seem to hold them to that, as seen in California's 1997 case of AMEX Life Assurance Company vs. Sloame Capital Corporation. A man who eventually died of AIDS personally attended the first part of the approval process and then substituted a much healthier impostor to take the medical exam. After three years of paying premiums, he died, and even though the switch was discovered by the carrier, the court ordered payment since the company was negligent in not noticing that his height and hair color had changed halfway through the approval process.

Special Operations

Varying by state, all other insurance claims are handled under one department entitled "Special Operations," with fraud investigators taking assigned cases as they come up, under the categories of life insurance fraud, renter's insurance fraud, scams relating to food products, arson, and slip and falls.

Arson

The determination of what causes a fire is probably a book in itself. I still don't know how they do that, but what I do know is what investigators look for to determine if the building or vehicle was torched. One major sign comes while taking an inventory of what was burned up. If everything of value was removed prior, including the family pet, investigators render the circumstances highly suspicious. Other curious factors are the financial state of the claimant (to determine motive), as well as whether there had been any recent increases in the coverage. Additionally, they check as to whether the claimant was out of town when the fire started; if the structure was for sale or was recently purchased; or if it was deteriorating or located in a declining neighborhood.

Slip and Falls

According to J.J. Jacobson, 95 percent of all slip and falls are bogus claims! The other 5 percent usually involve elderly people who are legitimately not as surefooted as they once were. Called *leg-breakers* or *flop artists*, these scamps are constantly falling over. Under different names, of course. The most common "culprits" are wet restaurant floors, broken pieces of tile, and tattered corners on a rug.

Food Products

In these claims, suspects bring their own chicken bones, bugs, etc., into a restaurant and plant them in the food. In the rusty nail scam, the fraud artist purposely cuts the inside of his mouth with a razor blade as he's chowing down. He screams and spits out the rusty item and loudly threatens to sue as the waiters scurry around, hiding him from other diners. Even if the café owner is suspicious, there's very little defense against such tactics.

Renter's Insurance

In another Gypsy exclusive, the perp is in his apartment or motel room when, inexplicably, a picture comes flying off the wall and hits the sleeping applicant on the noggin. Or down comes a ceiling fixture, walloping the claimant in the nose. Or the railing gives way and down he tumbles. Even in California, adjusters can link this paranormal commotion to no known seismic activity.

Pet Insurance

There aren't many pet insurance companies, but those that do exist are not immune to insurance fraud. One company received a note from a "Dr. Emanuelle" who said his "famale" (this could either mean *female* or *familya*, which is Romany for *family*) cat "slipped and fell" from the third-floor balcony of an apartment complex, and as a result received a "urinary track infection . . . and pain and suffering." Upon investigation it was discovered the $1400 bill was bogus; the cat's owner, "Dr. Emanuelle," was a doctor of unknown sorts; and the real-life vet who "signed" the claim had never heard of Dr. Emanuelle or the incident.

Bibliography

Abagnale, Frank W., Jr., with Stan Redding. *Catch Me If You Can*, New York: Grosset & Dunlap, Inc., 1980.

Easley, Bruce. *Biz-Op: How to Get Rich With "Business Opportunity" Frauds and Scams*. Port Townsend, Wash.: Loompanics Unlimited, 1994.

Ekman, Paul. *Telling Lies: Clues to Deceit in the Marketplace, Politics, and Marriage*. New York: W.W. Norton & Co., Inc., 1985.

Henderson, M. Allen. *Flimflam Man: How Con Games Work*. Boulder, Colo.: Paladin Press, 1985.

Henderson, M. Allen. *Money for Nothing: Rip-offs, Cons and Swindles*. Boulder, Colo.: Paladin Press, 1986.

Mott, Graham M. *How to Recognize and Avoid Scams, Swindles, and Rip-Offs*. Littleton, Colo.: Golden Shadows Press, 1993.

Randi, James. *Flim-Flam! Psychics, ESP, Unicorns, and Other Delusions*. Buffalo, N.Y.: Prometheus Books, 1982.

Santoro, Victor. *The Rip-Off Book*. Port Townsend, Wash.: Loompanics Unlimited, 1984.

Smith, Lindsay E., and Detective Bruce A. Walstad. *Sting Shift: The Street-Smart Cop's Handbook of Cons and Swindles*. Littleton, Colo.: Street-Smart Communications, 1989.

Steiner, Robert A. *Don't Get Taken! Bunco and Bunkum Exposed: How to Protect Yourself*. El Cerrito, Calif.: Wide-Awake Books, 1989.

Wright, Don. *Scam! Inside America's Con Artist Clans*. Elkhart, Ind.: Cottage Publications, 1996.

Index

A

Adoption scams, 36, 126-127
  policing agencies, 40
Antagonist, colorful, creating a, 28
Attorneys, as alternatives to
    policing, 41

B

Badge scam, 33, 180-182
Bail bond scheme, 33, 127
Bank examiner scam, 176-180
Bar games, 69-70
  See also Games
Better Business Bureau, as liaison
    with policing agencies, 41
Biz-op scams, 157-166
Blackmail, emotional, 27
Block hustle con, 35-37, 58-59
Books, where antisocials learn their
    trade, 32
Bunco, defined, 43-44
Business cons, 211-226

C

Card games, 67-68
  See also Games
Carnival
  games, 77-84
  layout, 72
  lingo, 72-76
  policing agencies, 40
Catch, 48-49, 56
  defined, 45
Celebrity con, 183-184
Chain letters, 148-150
Charges, criminal vs. civil, 9-11
Charity con, 140-141
  policing agencies, 40
Check kiting, 196
  policing agencies, 40
City inspector con, 141
Cold readings, psychic, 120-121
Come-on, the, as a component of a
    con, 18, 160-162
Commodity cons, 151-153
Con
  anatomy of a, 17-18
  elements of a, 12-20
  plotting a, 21-28

seven ingredients of a, 16-17
Con artist, 45
  See Gypsies; Perps
Con game
  lingo, 46-48
Con, big
  defined, 6-7
Con, short
  defined, 7, 46
  examples of, 188
Conpeople. *See* Con artist; Gypsies;
    Perps
Cons, types of
  adoption, 36
  advance fee, 153
  arson, 225
  assessor's kickback, 153-154
  at-home assembly, 163
  auto insurance, 219-222
  auto repairs, 35-37, 100
  badge, 33, 55, 180-182
  badger, 114
  bail bond, 33
  bait and switch, 35, 37, 40,
    141-143
  bank examiner, 1, 33, 176-179
  bar games, 69-70
  bartender's, 59-60
  Bible, 128
  Big Bill/Little Bill, 61-62
  biz-op, 35-36, 157-166
  block hustle, 35-37, 40, 58-59
  business, 211-226
  bust out, 212
  card games, 67-68
  caretaker, 2, 33, 102, 154
  carny, 35-37, 71-84
  cashier's five-for-ten boo-boo, 61
  celebrity, 183-184
  chain letter, 36, 148-150
  charity, 35, 40, 140-141
  charity boxes, 40, 163-164
  check kiting, 40, 196
  city inspector, 141
  clerk's sweaty palm holdout, 60
  combo, 62-63
  commodity, 151-153
  conning the clerk, 61-64
  conning the customer, 59-61

contest, 137
copper, 184-188
counterfeiting, 40, 189-203
country boy, 56
credential, 203-210
credit repair, 36
cruise, 213-215
cults, 36
dating, 115-116
delivery of non-ordered goods, 37
diamond ring, 50-51
direct-mail, 35, 37, 131-133,
    216-217
distributorship, 165
door-to-door, 40, 140-141,
    213-215
double play, 54-55
drop box, 188
drunken mitt, 68
809 phone numbers, 37, 140
E-mail blackmail, 215-216
entrapment, 114-115
equity purchaser, 154
faith healing, 36
forgery, 37, 40, 193-196
fortune-telling, 36, 95, 118-121
franchise, 166
gambling, 36, 40
glamour, 36, 167-174
gofer, 51-52
government warning, 216-217
guaranteed prize, 33, 136-137
gypsy, 40, 90-92
health and beauty, 40, 171-172
heirs on demand, 128-130
Hispanic heist, 127-128
home equity, 154-155
home improvement, 154
home invasion, 33, 102
home repairs, 33, 35-37, 101,
    106-107
horse racing, 65-67
identity theft, 35, 37, 204-210
Indian-head penny, 52
insurance, 37, 40, 103-104,
    110-111, 217-226
insurance, life, 222-225
Internet, 116-117, 215-216
investment, 37, 40, 144-156
Jamaican hustle, 52-53
job opportunity, 36, 156
Latin charity switch, 54
Latin lotto, 33, 54

little boy, 188
machine repair, 37
marked bill, 63-64
May-December romance, 133
metal sales, 37
metal theft, 101
miscount, 61
movies, making, 169-170
movies, reviewing, 170-171
Murphy man, 113-114
Nigerian letter, 182-183
office equipment, 212
one for five, 191
pay phone, 165
payoff, 66
PBX line, 212-213
pet, 36, 51, 226
phone, 196-198, 212-213
phony invoices, 37
pickpocketing, 37, 40
pigeon drop, 13-17, 33, 40, 48-50
Ponzi, 37, 40, 145-151
prison pen pal, 117-118
product demonstration, 141
products, food, 226
psychic, 36, 40, 97, 118-122
publishing, 171
put and take, 69
pyramid, 40, 144-151
real estate, 153-155
recovery, 137
refinancing, 154
religious, 140-141
rental, 155
renter's insurance, 226
retail, 40, 141-143 (See also Sales
    cons)
retirement, 36
Roscoe Duvall, 56-58
sales, 35, 107, 131-143 (See also
    Retail rip-offs)
shark, 68
shoplifting, 37, 91
shortchanging, 35-37, 40, 59-64
shoulder surfing, 37
slamming, 37, 40, 139
slips and falls, 226
smack, 69-70
solicitations disguised as
    invoices, 216
spiritual, 123-126
store diversion, 37, 90-91
street, 36-37, 40

stuffing envelopes, 164
sweepstakes, 36, 136
sweetheart, 2, 10-11, 27, 33,
    35-36, 40, 98-100, 112-113
talent-finders, 168-169
tear up, 68
telemarketing, 35, 37, 40,
    133-137, 139-140
Texas tornado, 56
Texas twist, 35, 56
three-card monte, 2, 36, 55-58
ticket teller's take it or leave
    it, 60
time-shares, 155
tool sales, 37
trailer sales, 35, 107
travel, 137-138
TV evangelists, 36, 41
unclaimed funds, 138-139
utility inspector, 33, 101, 109-110
vehicle sales, 35, 101
vending machines, 164-165
vendor's billfold, 60
wanna buy a watch?, 59
wire, 66
workers' compensation, 217-219
yellow page invoice, 216
See also Bunco, defined; Crimes,
    gypsy
Contest cons, 137
Copper con, 184-188
Counterfeiting, 37, 189-203
    policing agencies, 40
Crimes, gypsy
    by females, 95-100, 102-104
    by males, 100-104
    common denominators, 90-92
    policing agency, 40
    See also Gypsies
Criminals, career, 30

D
Direct-mail con. See Mail cons
Door-to-door cons, 140-141,
    213-215
    policing agencies, 40
Drag broads, 48, 180
    defined, 45

E
809 phone numbers, 37, 140
Emphasis, the, in a con, 19-20
Ending, happy, insuring a, 17

F
Faith healing, 126
Flimflam Man, 135
Forgery, 193-196
    policing agencies, 40
Fortune-telling, 36, 95, 118-121
Fraud
    home equity, 154-155
    insurance, 217-226
    personal check, 193
    phone, 196-198, 212-213
    policing agencies, 40
    telemarketing, 35, 37, 40,
        133-137, 139-140
    true party, 205
    See also Con; Scams; Schemes

G
Gambling stings, 65-70
    policing agencies, 40
Games, 46
    bar, 69-70
    card, 67-68
    carnival, 76-84
    of chance, 76-77
    flat, 77
    skill or science, 76
Glamour scams, 167-174
Gold investment cons, 40, 152-153
Guaranteed prize scam, 136-137
Gypsies, 85-111
    American, 92
    crimes committed by, 90-92,
        94-104
    European, 89-92
    history of, 88-89
    justice system, 88
    lingo, 87-88
    names and alias, 93-94
    social structure, 87

H
Handkerchief switch, 52-55
Heat, the, 40-41
    as protagonist, 28-29
    attorney general, 39
    beating the, gypsies, 104-105
    defined, 38
    district attorney, 39
    police, 39
    private enterprise, 41-42
Home equity fraud, 154-155

I

Identity cards, counterfeiting, 203
Identity theft, 35, 37, 204-210
Imposter cons, 175-188
Incarceration, where antisocials
    learn their trade, 31
Insurance fraud, 217-226
    policing agencies, 40
Internet, where antisocials learn their
    trade, 32
Internet cons, 116-117, 215-216
Investigative journalists, scam
    busting, 42

L

Lingo
    carny, 72-76
    con, 44-48
    gypsy, 87-88
    psychic, 118-122
Live one, as a prospective mark, 67
Lotteries, oil and gas, 151-152

M

Mail cons, 35, 37, 136-140, 216-217
Mark
    blow off the, 27
    calculating the stakes, 26
    delivering a return on investment,
        26
    gaining confidence of, 25
    keeping it quiet, 27
    pulling off the sting, 26-27
    putting on the send, 26, 58
    showing the money, 25, 45-46
    suitable, determining a, 25
    telling the tale, 25-26
    See also Lingo, con; Pigeons;
        Victims
Marks, easy, 34-37
Merchandise, counterfeiting,
    198-203
Mish roll, 5, 45-46
Money, show the, 45-46
    defined, 25
MOs, gypsy, 94
Motivation, as a component of a
    con, 18

N

National Association of Bunco
    Investigators (NABI), 42,
    86, 91

National Insurance Crime Bureau
    (NICB), 42
Nigerian letter scam, 182-183

O

Officia, gypsy, 96-97
    defined, 87
Opportunists, investment, 144-156

P

Perps, 112-130
    antisocial personality disorder of,
        29-30
    bank examiner's scam, 176
    body language, 32
    facial expressions, 32
    sweetheart scam, 98
    telemarketing fraud, 134-135
    where they learn their trade,
        31-32
Personal check fraud, 193
Phone fraud, 196-198, 212-213
Pigeon drop, 13-17, 33, 48-50
    policing agency, 40
Pigeons, 32-38
    personality traits of, 37-38
Pigeons, types of
    businesses, 37
    elderly, 33-34, 86, 92
    get-along guy, 35
    greedy son of a gun, 36-37
    men, 98-99
    needy Nellie, 36
    new kid on the block, 35
    random, 37
    stand-up person, 34-35
    stargazer, 35-36
    wild and crazy guy, 36
    See also Lingo, con; Mark;
        Victims
Pitch, telemarketing, 133-134
Plotting, cons
    case study, 21-28
    ten-step program for, 21-27
Policing agencies, 40-41
    See also Heat, the
Ponzi scheme, 37, 145-151
    policing agencies, 40
Pretext call, defined, 12-13
Private investigators, and confidence
    swindles, 42
Product demonstration con, 141

Professionals Against Confidence
  Crime, 42, 86
Props, con, 45-46, 48
Psychic surgery, 121-122
Psychics, 118-122
  cold readings by, 120-121
  history of, 119-120
  lingo, 118-119
  policing agencies, 40
  types of, 118-119
Psychotic. *See* Antisocial personality
  disorder
Publishers Clearing House
  Sweepstakes con, 136
Publishing scam, 171
Put on the send, defined, 26
Pyramid schemes, 144-151
  policing agencies, 40

R
Real estate rip-offs, 153-155
Recovery scams, 137
Religious con, 140-141
Retail rip-offs, 141-143
  policing agencies, 40
  See also Sales cons
Return on investment, delivering
  a, 26
Roper, role in a con, 67

S
Sales cons, 35, 107, 131-143
  See also Retail rip-offs
Scams
  account takeover, 204-205
  adoption, 36, 126-127
  badge, 33, 55, 180-182
  biz-op, 157-166
  busting, 42
  glamour, 167-174
  guaranteed prize, 136-137
  Nigerian letter, 182-183
  publishing, 171
  recovery, 137
  show business, 167-171
  sweetheart, 2, 10-11, 27, 33,
    35-36, 98-100, 112-113
  travel, 137-138
  unclaimed funds, 138-139
  See also Cons; Fraud; Schemes
Schemes
  bail bond, 33, 127

found money, 48-52
pyramid, 40, 144-151
  See also Con
Sex
  entrapment con, 114-115
  the promise of, 27, 99
Shill, as a component of a con,
  18, 67
Shortchanged, 61
Shortchanging, 59-64
  policing agency, 40
Show business scams, 167-171
Slamming, 139
  policing agency, 40
Society, where antisocials learn their
  trade, 31
Sociopath. *See* Antisocial
  personality disorder
Spiritual cons, 123-126
Stakes, calculating the, 26
Sting
  defined, 46
  gambling, 40, 65-70
  pulling off the, 26-27
  sweepstakes, 136
Sting Shift, 84, 120-121
Sweetheart scam, 2, 10-11, 27, 33,
  35-36, 98-100, 112-113
  policing agency, 40

T
Telemarketing cons, 35, 37,
  133-137, 139-140
  policing agencies, 41
Telling Lies, 32
Theft
  identity, 35, 37, 204-210
  metal, 101
Three-card monte, 2, 36, 55-58
Tramps, as con people, 85
Travel scams, 137-138
Travelers, as conpeople, 85, 105-111

U
Unclaimed funds scam, 138-139

V
Victims
  character development of, 28
  sweetheart scam, 98-99, 113
  See also Lingo, con; Mark;
    Pigeons